YORK NOT

General Editors: Professor A.N. Jeffares (*University of Stirling*) & Professor Suheil Bushrui (*American University of Beirut*)

Henry Fielding

JOSEPH ANDREWS

Notes by Bruce King

BA (COLUMBIA) PH D (LEEDS)
Professor of English,
University of Canterbury

LONGMAN
YORK PRESS

YORK PRESS
Immeuble Esseily, Place Riad Solh, Beirut

LONGMAN GROUP UK LIMITED
Longman House, Burnt Mill, Harlow,
Essex CM20 2JE, England
Associated companies, branches and representatives
throughout the world

First published 1981
Sixth impression 1993

ISBN 0-582-78174-4

Produced by Longman Singapore Publishers Pte Ltd
Printed in Singapore

Contents

Part 1

Introduction

The life of Henry Fielding

Henry Fielding was born on 22 April 1707 at Sharpham Park, near Glastonbury in Somerset. His was a landowning family and as a boy he lived on a farm at East Stour, Dorset. At the age of twelve he went to Eton, where he remained until 1724. During 1728 he published a satiric poem, *The Masquerade*, and his first play, *Love in Several Masques*, was produced. During the same year he enrolled as a student of letters in the University of Leyden, in the Netherlands. In 1729 he left Leyden to go to London where he began a career as a professional dramatist. In 1734 he eloped with and married Charlotte Cradock.

Although now primarily known as a novelist, Fielding was a major dramatist of the early eighteenth century. Voltaire and other commentators of the age compared him with the great French dramatist Molière (1622–73). George Bernard Shaw claimed that Fielding was 'the greatest practising dramatist' in English between Shakespeare and the nineteenth century. His plays are witty, satirical, comical, topical and realistic. The best-known are *The Author's Farce* (1730), *Rape Upon Rape* (1730), *The Tragedy of Tragedies; or, The Life and Death of Tom Thumb the Great* (1731), *The Welsh Opera* (1731), *The Modern Husband* (1732), *The Covent Garden Tragedy* (1732), *The Miser* (1733), *Don Quixote in England* (1734), *Pasquin* (1736), *The Historical Register for the Year 1736* (1737). Many of the plays are examples of Fielding's love of parodying what he considered absurd theatrical and literary conventions. *The Tragedy of Tragedies*, set at the court of King Arthur, made fun of the Restoration heroic drama made popular by John Dryden (1631–1700) in the late seventeenth century. *The Covent Garden Tragedy* burlesqued the sentimental tragedy of the early eighteenth century.

Besides making fun of the existing theatre repertoire, Fielding satirised the leading politicians and public figures of his day. The Whig government in power between 1721 and 1742 was led by Sir Robert Walpole (1676–1745), a still controversial figure, sometimes seen as the first modern English prime minister, but more often viewed as a ruthlessly corrupt party boss who stayed in office by rewarding his followers and punishing those who opposed him. To many writers of the age Walpole represented what was wrong with England. He was satirised by Jonathan Swift (1667–1745) in *Gulliver's Travels* (1726), by John Gay (1685–1732) in *The Beggar's Opera* (1728) and by Samuel Johnson (1709–84) in *London* (1738).

Fielding's satire on Walpole, King George II and the Queen resulted in the Theatrical Licensing Act (1737), which censored the stage. Only two theatres were permitted to remain open. Fielding's Little Theatre was closed. He was driven to find other means of livelihood and soon became a novelist.

After the passage of the Theatrical Licensing Act Fielding began to study law at the Middle Temple. In 1740 he was admitted to the bar. He also worked as a journalist and during 1739–41 edited *The Champion* for the political opposition to Walpole.

Samuel Richardson's (1689–1761) novel *Pamela: or, Virtue Rewarded* appeared in 1740 and immediately became a sensation. In little more than a year six editions were published. Richardson's story of a virtuous servant girl protecting her chastity against her wealthy employer, which resulted in her triumph over him and their marriage, was highly praised as an example of moral purity. Several writers produced continuations, burlesques and parodies of *Pamela*. Fielding's parody, *An Apology for the Life of Mrs Shamela Andrews* (1741), treated the chastity of Richardson's heroine as a debasement of Christian virtue to calculation. Whereas Richardson's sub-title, *Virtue Rewarded*, pointed to a relationship between remaining sexually pure and advancement in the world, Fielding saw such profitable virtue as dishonest and hypocritical; such behaviour was a financial transaction having little to do with goodness of heart or spirit. Moreover, Fielding felt that Richardson's novel was clumsy, pretentious and absurd. He was especially annoyed by the various defences and self-congratulatory letters Richardson included in later editions of *Pamela*. *Shamela* was an attempt at literary and moral good sense. *Shamela* also made fun of *An Apology for the Life of Mr Colley Cibber, Comedian* (1740), a then famous autobiography by a well known actor and Poet Laureate (1730) of the early part of the century (1671–1757). Cibber is King Dunce in Alexander Pope's (1688–1749) *The Dunciad* (1743).

During 1741 Fielding rather surprisingly stopped supporting the opposition to Walpole and wrote a satiric pamphlet, *The Opposition: a vision*. Although the actual causes of Fielding's disenchantment with the Patriots are not clear, it appears, from his writing, that he felt the opposition had become as hypocritical and unprincipled as those in power. Subsequently Fielding's work shows disapproval of both the administration and the opposition. Walpole fell from power in 1742.

In 1742 Fielding published *The History of the Adventures of Joseph Andrews, And of his Friend Mr Abraham Adams. Written in Imitation of the Manner of Cervantes.* The only major English novels before *Joseph*

Andrews were Daniel Defoe's (1660–1731) *Robinson Crusoe* (1719) and *Moll Flanders* (1722) and Richardson's *Pamela*. Although *Joseph Andrews* was an immediate success with the reading public, it received little published contemporary literary criticism and many educated people were puzzled by its mixture of comedy and seriousness. Dr George Cheyne wrote to Richardson: 'It will entertain none but Porters or Watermen.' The poet Thomas Gray (1716–71) wrote to a friend that *Joseph Andrews* lacked 'invention' but praised the characters and social observations. William Shenstone (1714–63) thought the character of Parson Adams 'tedious' and the book mostly '*unnatural* and *unhumorous*'. Others enjoyed the variety, wit, morality and good sense of the novel and commented upon the 'spirit of benevolence' which runs throughout the book. Readers were particularly struck by the good-natured but eccentric character of Parson Adams, who advises and accompanies Joseph Andrews. Fielding's concept of Parson Adams was based on the Old Testament patriarch Abraham, on Miguel de Cervantes's (1547–1616) knight, Don Quixote, and on William Young (1702–57), an eccentric curate in East Stour, the village in Dorset where Fielding lived as a child.

Fielding was soon praised for using characters and places that existed and were representative of real life in contrast to the charmed warriors, crystal palaces and winged horses that previously filled prose and epic romances. Critics commented favourably on Fielding's style in *Joseph Andrews* and especially on his use of the mock-heroic to ridicule the bombast and inflated writing that was common to the romance. They found the chapter titles of the novel unusual and amusing. Fielding was said to have shown the ruling passions of men, their foibles and their oddities. Arthur Murphy, in *An Essay on the Life and Genius of Henry Fielding* (1762), praised Fielding's sense of the ridiculous. Fielding shows the inconsistencies that flow from vanity, from affectation and from hypocrisy. In *Joseph Andrews* the man of pretences usually turns out to be the very reverse of what he would appear.

Joseph Andrews was followed by *The Life of Mr Jonathan Wild the Great* (1743), a satiric novel which again alluded to Sir Robert Walpole. *Jonathan Wild* was included in the three volumes of *Miscellanies* (1743), also containing various essays, poems and plays. In 1744 Fielding's wife died. The Jacobite rebellion of 1745 threatened the government. The young pretender to the throne, Charles Edward Stuart, returned to Scotland and those who supported him marched through the north of England as far south as Derby. They were defeated in 1746. During 1745–6 Fielding edited *The True Patriot*, in defence of the ruling Hanoverians. In 1747 he married again, this time Mary Daniel, his housekeeper. The next year he edited *The Jacobite's Journal*, also in defence of the Hanoverians. His novels *Tom Jones* (1749) and *Amelia*

(1751) were written during a time when Fielding became increasingly involved with legal and social problems. He had been empowered to act as a magistrate for the district of Westminster, London, in 1748, and in 1749 was commissioned magistrate for the County of Middlesex. His *Enquiry into the Causes of the Late Increase of Robbers* (1751) was followed by *A Proposal for Making Effectual Provision for the Poor* (1753). In 1754 he became seriously ill. He travelled to Portugal, where he died on 8 October 1754. His *Journal of a Voyage to London* (1755) was published after his death.

A note on the text

Joseph Andrews was published in 1742 in two volumes by Andrew Millar (1706–68), a well known London bookseller. Millar had a reputation for honesty and generosity in his treatment of authors. According to one literary legend, Millar offered eight times more for the novel than Fielding expected. Fielding was so stunned that he could not answer coherently and the publisher assumed that the author was insulted or trying to bargain. Even before *Joseph Andrews* was published it had created interest among those who looked forward to what they expected to be another parody of *Pamela*. The book was an immediate success and within a few months a second edition was needed; within three years over six thousand copies of the novel were sold. The second edition was 'Revised and Corrected with *Alterations* and *Additions* by the *AUTHOR*'. Other editions followed (1743, 1748, 1751). Translations appeared in France, Germany, Italy and Denmark.

In the twentieth century *Joseph Andrews* has often been republished. The standard modern edition is that edited by Martin C. Battestin, Oxford University Press, 1967, as part of the *Wesleyan Edition of the Works of Henry Fielding*. Douglas Brooks's edition, Oxford University Press, 1970, is indebted to that of Battestin. In compiling these Notes I have used R.F. Brissenden's widely available edition, Penguin Books, Harmondsworth, 1977, 1978, which also follows Battestin, except in minor matters of capitalisation, spelling and punctuation.

Part 2

Summaries
of JOSEPH ANDREWS

A general summary

Joseph Andrews, the supposed brother of the chaste heroine of Richardson's novel *Pamela*, is a servant of Lady Booby. He refuses her advances as he loves a childhood friend, Fanny, and as he wishes to follow Pamela's chaste example and the teaching of Parson Adams. Dismissed from employment by Lady Booby, Joseph travels from London through the countryside to see Fanny. On his way he meets Parson Adams, the learned but eccentric clergyman who is his moral guide and who will accompany him during the journey. After many adventures and coincidences Joseph is reunited with Fanny, who, having heard of his troubles, has been seeking him. They wish to marry, but Adams objects that they have not yet fulfilled Church law by publicly announcing their intentions three times.

Adams, Joseph and Fanny continue to travel towards Adams's parish, which is also the country seat of the Boobys. Lady Booby, who has also returned home, jealously attempts to stop Joseph from marrying Fanny. Meanwhile Pamela, by remaining chaste, has caused her employer, the nephew of Lady Booby, to marry her. Pamela, however, objects to Joseph's marrying Fanny, a servant girl of unknown parentage. Mr and Mrs Andrews arrive and it is now discovered that Fanny is their daughter, who as a baby was stolen by gypsies, who left a baby boy in her place. Joseph is found to be the son of Mr Wilson, a rich gentleman from whom he was stolen. The two lovers, having now fulfilled Church law and overcome objections to their marriage, live happily ever after.

Detailed summaries

Joseph Andrews consists of a preface followed by four books divided into a total of sixty-four chapters. As each chapter is prefaced by a short, often humorous summary, and is rich in material, only the main matters of interest can be discussed in this critical analysis. (As the Penguin, Oxford, Methuen and other standard editions contain full notes, the glossary and commentary will mention only significant points or matters not found in most editions used by students.)

Preface

The preface distinguishes Fielding's novel from such well known literary forms as the serious epic in verse, the romance and the burlesque. *Joseph Andrews* is a comic romance, a comic epic poem in prose. It has the length and comprehensiveness of an epic, but differs from serious romance in being 'light' and treating of the ridiculous. Although the style sometimes includes parodies or burlesque imitations, the novel is not a burlesque, as the characters are based on those found in real life: 'life every where furnishes an accurate observer with the ridiculous'. The ridiculous results from affectation, vanity and hypocrisy. Natural imperfections should not be the object of derision; but when ugliness pretends to be beautiful then what would otherwise move our compassion will raise our mirth.

NOTES AND GLOSSARY:

a different idea of romance: Fielding is aware that the novel as a form is in its infancy and that his blending of seriousness with humour and comedy is likely to confuse his readers. Citing the classic work of literary criticism, Aristotle's *Poetics*, he claims to derive his kind of prose fiction from a lost Greek satirical epic. (The epic was long considered the highest form of literature.) He explains how his comic epic differs from the romantic prose tales concerning noble lives and the various burlesques which treated of low subject matter in an elevated style. He claims that there are similarities between his treatment of character and the caricatures done by his friend William Hogarth (1697–1764), the well known realistic painter and engraver. (The preface, along with Book I, 1; Book II, 1 and Book III, 1, are the foundations of Fielding's theory of the novel. These sections should be studied carefully)

Book I Chapter 1

The narrator, who should not necessarily be seen as Henry Fielding himself, speaks of the moral purpose of actual examples to good behaviour. While the example of a good man is a better lesson than a good book, the lives of the best men are little known. In communicating models to the reader a biography can be even more useful to mankind than the great person whose life is recorded. The reader is improved by a mixture of instruction and entertainment.

The narrator then ironically mentions two recent books as admirable patterns of behaviour. *An Apology for the Life of Mr Colley Cibber, Comedian* (1740) shows the wrongness of those who fear shame of their reputation. Of Richardson's novel, *Pamela: or, Virtue Rewarded* (1741), the narrator does not bother to comment beyond saying that the author's various prefaces to the novel explain themselves. With tongue in cheek the narrator says that his Joseph Andrews is the brother of Pamela and has kept in mind the pattern of his sister's virtues. He is an example of 'male-chastity'.

NOTES AND GLOSSARY:

Of writing Lives in general: despite the humorous and ironic manner of the narrator, Fielding continues to offer his theory of fiction. Examples are morally instructive; the writer offers models of behaviour. He mocks those who claim the great authors of the past are 'obsolete'; he absurdly praises as examples of useful modern literature various cheap romances of his own time. (Colley Cibber's *Apology* and Richardson's *Pamela* are further discussed in Part 3 of these Notes)

Book I Chapter 2

The parentage of Joseph Andrews is given as if he were a hero. But, unable to trace Joseph's ancestry through past generations, the narrator claims that it 'is sufficiently certain' that he had 'as many ancestors' as any other man. By the time he was ten and could read and write, Joseph was apprenticed to Sir Thomas Booby, for whom he took care of dogs and horses. His voice was so excellent that he was moved from working in the fields to the stables. At the age of seventeen he caught the eye of Lady Booby who wanted him for her personal servant. Mr Abraham Adams, the curate, was surprised at his religious knowledge.

Book I Chapter 3

Several character sketches follow. Parson Abraham Adams is an excellent scholar, who is good-natured but ignorant of the ways of the world. 'Simplicity' is his character. This makes him a good country parson, but results in a small income which is not enough to live well with his wife and six children.

Parson Adams is surprised that Joseph can answer questions about the New Testament. Joseph learned to read and write from his father. While in Sir Thomas Booby's family he has spent his leisure time reading morally educational and religious books. He is satisfied with the state of life in which he finds himself. He does not envy others.

Sir Thomas seldom sees Parson Adams; he values people only according to their wealth or appearance. Lady Booby considers the country people brutes.

Mrs Slipslop, 'the waiting-gentlewoman', has respect for Adams, but wants him to accept her superior knowledge of theology. She likes to use jargon, which often she does not understand. Adams recommends to her that he should take on Joseph's education so that the young man can advance in life. She replies that Lady Booby is going to London and will want to take Joseph with her.

NOTES AND GLOSSARY:

to improve his talent: the parable of the talents is often alluded to by Parson Adams. See the Bible, Matthew 25:14–30

Book I Chapter 4

In London Joseph follows the fashions, but avoids gambling, drinking and other vices. Although he is handsome, he remains uncorrupted. He spends his leisure time on music. Lady Booby, who considers Joseph lacking in spirit, now finds his city manners encouraging. She holds hands with him, has him bring messages to her bedroom, and leers at him. While Joseph remains chaste despite such temptations, London gossip suggests that he has become Lady Booby's lover.

Book I Chapter 5

When Sir Thomas Booby dies, his wife pretends to mourn, but in fact plays cards with her friends for six days. On the seventh day she attempts to seduce Joseph. Disappointed that he has not made advances to her, she assumes he is inhibited by fear and respect. She now tempts him; she says that he should not be dissuaded from love by the inequality of his social station or by fear of being rejected. When Joseph does not make love to her, Lady Booby says he is either a fool or pretends to be, so as to avoid what she is offering. She orders him out of her room. What Joseph sees as loyalty to her honour and that of her husband, Lady Booby sees as a rejection of herself.

NOTES AND GLOSSARY:

but on the seventh: an ironic echo of the Bible, Genesis 2:2: 'And on the seventh day God ended his work which he had made; and he rested on the seventh day from all his work which he had made.'

Joseph:	in Genesis 39:7–20 Joseph resists the advances of Potiphar's wife: 'his master's wife cast her eyes upon Joseph, and she said, Lie with me. But he refused.' Joseph was taken as a model of male chastity

Book I Chapter 6

Joseph writes a letter to his sister Pamela complaining that Lady Booby ordered him to sit by her when she was in bed and held his hand. He wishes to leave the house for another job before he is dismissed. London appears to him a bad place.

After he has written the letter, Joseph is approached by Mrs Slipslop, who also desires him for a lover. An ugly old woman, Mrs Slipslop has been without a lover for so long that she is no longer afraid of ruining her reputation or damaging her soul. Just as Joseph's modesty insults Lady Booby's advances, so he insults Mrs Slipslop by offering her respect. 'I have always loved you as well as if you had been my own mother.' Although insulted by the truth that she might be old enough to be Joseph's mother, Mrs Slipslop plans to make love violently to Joseph. He is saved by the ringing of Lady Booby's bell.

NOTES AND GLOSSARY:

Since I received your letter: Richardson's *Pamela* is an epistolary novel, that is, it is partly told in the form of letters. After Mr B—'s wife dies, Pamela becomes the object of her employer's attempts at seduction and rape

Parson Williams: the full title of Fielding's *An Apology for the Life of Mrs Shamela Andrews* includes 'a full Account of all that passed between her and Parson Arthur Williams; whose Character is represented in a manner something different from what he bears in *Pamela*'. Williams, a harmless parson in Richardson's novel, becomes Pamela's lover in *Shamela*

As when a hungry tygress: a mock-heroic simile

Book I Chapter 7

Feeling rejected, Lady Booby wants to rid herself of Joseph. She calls Mrs Slipslop to her room. The two disappointed women discuss the young man. Mrs Slipslop falsely claims he is a drunkard, gambler and a lewd rascal who has made a chambermaid pregnant. Lady Booby tells her to dismiss Joseph and the maid from their jobs. Having gone too far,

Mrs Slipslop begins to defend Joseph. Lady Booby, angry with Joseph but in love with him, acts confusedly and changes her mind several times before saying she wants to see him immediately. She plans to insult then dismiss him.

Book I Chapter 8

Joseph, who is now twenty-one years old, good looking and well dressed, is interviewed by Lady Booby concerning his supposed wicked misbehaviour with the maids in the house. She says that while others would dismiss him for his offences she has compassion for his youth. She implies that he could kiss her; the granting of a kiss might lead to further liberties. Joseph says he hopes that if he were kissed he could control his emotions and keep acting virtuously. Lady Booby explodes at this proclamation of male virtue: 'Did ever mortal hear of a man's virtue!' Joseph appeals to the virtuous conduct of his sister Pamela as his example; Lady Booby exclaims at her relative, Squire Booby, ever putting up with Pamela. She orders Joseph out of her sight and out of the house.

NOTES AND GLOSSARY:

Now the rake Hesperus: a comic description of the morning, parodying the elevated classical style

statue of surprize: a stereotyped acting gesture; the actor stands motionless like a statue, with his eyes open in amazement

Book I Chapter 9

Lady Booby summons Mrs Slipslop and tells her that Joseph is to be immediately dismissed. Slipslop, having listened through the keyhole to the previous scene with Joseph, tells her mistress to make up her mind instead of continually dismissing and rehiring Joseph. Knowing Lady Booby's desire for Joseph, Slipslop no longer fears her and instead mocks her air of moral outrage. Lady Booby, thinking Joseph has revealed her passion to Slipslop, tells her to find another job. But soon Lady Booby becomes worried about her reputation, without which she would not be invited to play cards and partake in other social events. She decides that while Joseph is to be dismissed she will rehire Slipslop who, having made up her mind that it is better to keep a job than search for another, accepts reconciliation.

Book I Chapter 10

Joseph writes a letter to Pamela lamenting that Lady Booby has fallen in love with him. 'She has a mind to ruin me.' In the letter he praises chastity and resolves to protect his virtue. He pledges himself to imitate Pamela's chastity. Accepting his dismissal from service, he receives his remaining wages from the steward, Peter Pounce. Pounce, by lending money at usurious rates, has used his position to become rich. Joseph leaves the house with little money or clothing late that night.

NOTES AND GLOSSARY:

you will have grace: Fielding associated Pamela's piety with the Methodist stress on grace and faith as more necessary for salvation than good works. 'Grace' is slipped into the letter two paragraphs previously

Book I Chapter 11

Instead of seeking the protection of his parents or Pamela, Joseph leaves London for Lady Booby's country seat. In that parish lives Fanny, a beautiful but poor girl brought up by Sir Thomas's family. She and Joseph have been in love for many years, but have not married as Parson Adams advised them to wait until they had sufficient money and experience to live comfortably.

During a storm Joseph takes shelter in an inn. Another traveller offers to let Joseph use his extra horse as they are going in the same direction.

Book I Chapter 12

The two travellers reach an inn. Joseph continues his journey on foot. He is attacked and beaten unconscious by two robbers who take his clothes and money. After a time a stage-coach comes past. The passengers uncharitably do not want to stop to help. Some fear they also will be robbed. Others object that Joseph is naked; others say that if he dies they will have more trouble. None of the rich passengers will lend Joseph clothing, but the postillion gives him his own coat so that he can enter the coach. Immediately afterwards the coach is robbed. Eventually the coach arrives at an inn where Betty, the maid, provides a shirt and a bed for Joseph. Mr Tow-wouse, the owner of the inn, and his wife argue over the charity Betty has given.

NOTES AND GLOSSARY:

postillion: the man who rides on one of the leading horses; he is therefore outside the coach

Book I Chapter 13

At the inn Joseph is visited by a doctor who speaks medical jargon and tells him to make his will. Barnabas, the local clergyman, tells Joseph that this world is carnal and he must place all his hopes of happiness in Heaven. Instead Joseph's thoughts are on Fanny. The clergyman offers further advice about forgiving those who rob us. Joseph, who is suffering from a fever, wants tea, but is told there is none. The preacher, however, is given tea and punch to drink. Later Betty brings Joseph some tea.

NOTES AND GLOSSARY:

must be done by grace: the Methodists, and Richardson, believed in the superiority of grace to good works. Just as in the novel self-interest is contrasted to charity, so grace and faith are contrasted to charity. Fielding believes that Christianity must be expressed in charity towards others

Book I Chapter 14

A stranger enters the inn. Mr Tow-wouse complains to him of Joseph's having been left at the inn. The stranger has read the classical works of medicine in their original Greek. One of the thieves is caught and Joseph's small gold coin is found in his possession. Joseph's clothing is also found. The stranger turns out to be Parson Adams. After some discussion it is decided to keep the thief at the inn overnight and take him before a justice of the peace the next day.

Book I Chapter 15

Mrs Tow-wouse thinks that Joseph might be a gentleman and starts to treat him better. The clergyman, Barnabas, and the surgeon unsuccessfully try to obtain the gold piece from Joseph to use as evidence. The two argue with each other over fine points of the law of evidence. Parson Adams is on his way to London to attempt to sell his sermons. Joseph, given some food, begins to recover.

Book I Chapter 16

The thief is left unguarded and escapes during the night. The constable is suspected of having been bribed to enable him to escape. Mr Tow-wouse fears that as the landlord he could be accused of helping the thief to escape. Adams, who is running out of money, wants to borrow some from the landlord, and offers his nine volumes of sermons as security. Barnabas tells Adams that no one reads sermons. The doctor claims credit for Joseph's recovery. While Joseph's wounds are healing three days pass. A friend of Barnabas arrives at the inn.

NOTES AND GLOSSARY:

reward: the reward for capturing a highwayman if he was convicted was £40 and any goods on him

make up a sum: obliged to pay by a certain date

peppered: infected by venereal disease

Tillotson's sermons: John Tillotson (1630–94), Archbishop of Canterbury, was a leading Latitudinarian, famous for the clear, easy, logical style of his sermons. He preached the need for good works and Christian behaviour in society

Book I Chapter 17

Barnabas introduces his friend, a bookseller, to Adams. The bookseller says that the trade is overstocked with sermons. He would, however, take the sermons with him to London and send his opinion about them later. Adams, Barnabas and the bookseller argue over the importance of faith and works. Adams believes that faith is shown in works. They are interrupted by a loud quarrel between Mrs Tow-wouse and Betty, who has been found in bed with Mr Tow-wouse. Mrs Tow-wouse attempts to hit Betty, but Adams prevents her. Betty escapes.

NOTES AND GLOSSARY:

bookseller: in the seventeenth and eighteenth centuries, booksellers were also usually publishers

Whitfield or Westley: George Whitefield (1714–70) and John Wesley (1703–91) were Church reformers associated with Methodism

30th of January: Charles I was executed on 30 January 1649

one of Whitfield's: George Whitefield's sermons were in great demand at the time

Toland, Woolston: John Toland (1670–1722) and Thomas Woolston (1670–1733), well known free-thinkers or Deists. Toland was famous for his *Christianity Not Mysterious* (1696)

A Plain Account: published in 1735 by Benjamin Hoadley (1676–1761), a Latitudinarian bishop who claimed that the mass is a memorial of Christ's death which reminds Christians of their moral duties

Book I Chapter 18

The background to the previous chapter is explained. Betty, who is generous, attractive and has had many affairs with men, falls in love with Joseph. When she attempts to make love to him, he rejects her. Angry, she allows herself to be taken to bed by the landlord, whose wife discovers them. Betty is discharged from their employment.

NOTES AND GLOSSARY:

the western circuit: judges travelled to hold court locally. The western circuit was from Southampton through Dorchester and Exeter to Bristol

Book II Chapter 1

Book II opens with a playfully ironic essay on the reasons for dividing a work of literature into books and chapters. In defending this practice the narrator makes fun of other trades which have their 'secrets' such as prime ministering and tailoring, and of various literary and publishing practices. Using a metaphoric comparison of a story to a journey, the spaces between chapters are inns or resting-places; blank pages are stages in a journey; and chapter titles allow the reader to skip what he does not like. The 'art of dividing', which is part of 'the science of authoring', has the advantage of enabling a reader to begin again in the same place without having to turn down the pages of a book to mark where he left off.

Book II Chapter 2

Adams is ready to leave the inn to sell his sermons in London while Joseph will go to Fanny. Adams, however, accidentally leaves the sermons behind. He takes this as a sign that he should return to his parish instead of going to London. With one horse between them Joseph and Adams take turns to ride and walk. The rider will, after going a distance, tie the horse to a tree and then proceed on foot until the other has caught up. Joseph at the last moment is detained at the inn because of an unexpected debt for horse feed. Meanwhile Adams, who has gone ahead on foot, waits for Joseph at an alehouse.

Book II Chapter 3

At the alehouse, two men enter, laughing about a horse being detained at another inn. Adams realises it is his horse. A stage-coach arrives with Mrs Slipslop. She has met Joseph and paid for the horse. When Joseph arrives it is decided that he should keep the horse while Adams rides in the coach with Mrs Slipslop. She and Adams discuss Lady Booby's passion for Joseph. A passenger in the coach begins to tell a story about Leonora, a fashionable young woman.

Book II Chapter 4

Leonora, the attractive daughter of a gentleman, loves gaiety. She is engaged to be married to Horatio, a young, handsome gentleman of a good family. A fortnight before their wedding Leonora sees a fashionable coach with six horses pass her window and declares 'O I am in love with that equipage!' At a ball she meets the owner of the coach, Bellarmine, who wears fine French clothing. Leonora is flattered by his attention and by being the envy of the other women present. She dances with Bellarmine until six in the morning. The next afternoon he declares his love. She is so impressed by his refinement, gallantry, French fashions and what she assumes to be his fortune, that she quarrels with Horatio, who challenges the Frenchman to a duel and wounds him. Leonora blames herself in case Bellarmine should die; hopelessly in love, she visits him, despite the effect on her reputation.

NOTES AND GLOSSARY:

The History of Leonora: the story concerning Leonora is one of the two long digressions in the novel obliquely related to its main themes of love and charity. By eighteenth-century canons of taste, it is a moralistic set piece and also provides variety to the main narrative

the smarts: the gay blades, or fashionable young men

Book II Chapter 5

The story of Leonora is interrupted when the coach arrives at an inn, where Adams finds Joseph with a sore leg as a result of being thrown from the parson's weak-kneed horse. The innkeeper enters and quarrels with his wife for anointing Joseph's leg instead of preparing food for the coach passengers. Adams and the innkeeper quarrel and fight. The wife tosses a pan of hog's blood in Adams's face. Mrs Slipslop enters the kitchen and joins the battle. Some travellers separate the combatants.

As they prepare to leave the inn, Miss Grave-airs, one of the passengers, argues against admitting a footman, Joseph, into the stage-coach. By coincidence, Miss Grave-airs's father rides by and asks his daughter to accompany him in his own coach. After she departs the stage-coachman says that the father was himself once a postillion, but now being made a steward he acts like a great gentleman.

Book II Chapter 6

As the coach continues its journey the story of Leonora is concluded. Leonora has become Bellarmine's mistress and lives with him. Soon everyone talks of it. When Bellarmine asks her father what dowry will follow from their marriage he is told that he will receive nothing. Bellarmine immediately returns to France, blaming the father for preventing the marriage. Because of her reputation, Leonora is unable to marry anyone else and is unhappy for the rest of her life. Horatio, who has since become rich, still sighs at the mention of her name, and never speaks ill of her.

Book II Chapter 7

After the story of Leonora finishes, Joseph sees Adams walking ahead. The absent-minded parson forgot his horse and left it at the inn. They try to catch up with him but Adams walks faster than the coach travels. Outdistancing the coach and taking a wrong turning, Adams sits down to rest and hears a gunshot. Soon a gentleman appears with a dead partridge. The sportsman says that soldiers quartered in the neighbourhood have killed most of the game. He complains about the army and its failures abroad.

Book II Chapter 8

The parson tells the gentleman about his past. Adams has sacrificed advancement of his career for his principles. He refused to influence his nephew's political opinions in an election and as a result he lost his curacy. He has since been returned to his curacy but has not advanced to a better position because of the opposition of Lady Booby, who feels that his clothes and manners are not suitable. Adams has a son, nearly thirty years old, whom the bishop has refused to ordain because he is not a university graduate.

Book II Chapter 9

Adams and the gentleman continue to speak of bravery and patriotism. Learning that he has missed the stage-coach, Adams accepts the gentleman's invitation to go to his house. On the way they hear a woman shrieking. The 'man of courage' is frightened and leaves, but Adams goes to the rescue of the woman. He fights with her attempted ravisher and knocks him unconscious. The woman says that she was travelling towards London when she met a stranger who promised to guide her and then attempted to violate her.

NOTES AND GLOSSARY:

As a game-cock: a mock-heroic simile, humorously appropriate for introducing the 'low-life' battle between Adams and the attempted ravisher

---

Book II Chapter 10

It is now dark. While Adams decides what to do next, several young men appear. The parson tells them what happened. The villain has meanwhile regained consciousness and seeing that he cannot escape accuses Adams and the woman of attempting to murder him! Immediately the young men seize Adams and the woman as probable criminals. They argue over the reward they will get. While being escorted to the justice of the peace, Adams discovers that the woman he rescued is Fanny, Joseph's beloved. Hearing of Joseph's trouble she immediately went in search of him.

NOTES AND GLOSSARY:

Fanny: the coincidence is not very probable. Like other coincidences in the novel, it should be seen within the conventions of Renaissance literature which often placed high value on surprise and an intricate artifice or craftsmanship. The contrivance is thus a somewhat tongue-in-cheek parody of coincidences in earlier pastorals and romances

---

Book II Chapter 11

The parson and Fanny are taken before the justice who immediately treats them as proven criminals. A crowd gathers and insults them. They do not believe Adams is a clergyman and accuse him of stealing his cassock. The justice is going to commit them to prison for several months to await trial when one of the company suddenly recognises Adams and has him released. Meanwhile the real criminal has escaped. The justice, who a few minutes before was going to send Adams and Fanny to prison without hearing any evidence, now tells the company that he will send them all to prison if they do not capture the escaped criminal within a few days. Adams and the justice start to dispute over the law. Adams argues that on the evidence he should not have been set free. Fanny meets someone who knows where Joseph is; she and Adams leave the magistrate.

NOTES AND GLOSSARY:

and his cups: it will be noticed that the law is often portrayed as inefficient, unreliable and corrupt

Book II Chapter 12

They go a mile but are forced to stop at an alehouse because of a violent storm. Fanny is described to the reader. She is nineteen, tall, 'delicately shaped', large breasted, full hipped and has chestnut brown hair. Adams is reading his Aeschylus when he hears a song. Fanny faints. The singer is Joseph who on entering the room clasps Fanny in his arms and kisses her. After a display of emotion Fanny becomes aware of others in the room. She pushes Joseph from her and curtsies to Mrs Slipslop who refuses the greeting and leaves the room.

NOTES AND GLOSSARY:

The Song: it is a typical song of the late seventeenth century. It appears artificial and filled with classical allusions and diction, but its conclusion depends on the well known pun on expiring ('to die', 'to experience sexual bliss'), and the sexual *double entendre* of the word 'pressing'

Joseph Andrews himself: yet another coincidental meeting! This chapter includes the first description of Fanny and shows the passion which she and Joseph feel for each other. The song offers a parallel to the situation in the scene

Aeschylus lay expiring: Fielding repeats the word from the last stanza of the song to ensure that the reader is aware of the strong feelings which the young couple have for each other

Book II Chapter 13

The narrator satirically comments that Mrs Slipslop's refusal to acknowledge Fanny, although they lived in the same house for many years, is an imitation of fashionable behaviour; 'high people' never admit they know social inferiors. Slipslop says she 'can't remember all the inferior servants in our family', and calls Fanny a wench and a slut. When Joseph refuses to leave without Fanny, Slipslop, who is jealous, angrily departs in her coach. Adams, Joseph and Fanny do not go to bed. Adams falls asleep in his chair. The young couple speak of love, kiss and embrace. They wake Adams, requesting him to perform a wedding on the spot. He, however, insists that they follow the church regulations and wait until their intentions have been publicly announced three times.

It is now morning; when they start to leave they find they have not enough money to pay their bill at the inn. Adams decides to ask a local parson for some money.

NOTES AND GLOSSARY:

gives Octavia: in John Dryden's *All for Love* (1678), Act III, it is Octavia, rather than Cleopatra, who examines the other woman with disapproval: 'I would view nearer/That face, which has so long usurped my right.' As elsewhere in the novel Fielding alludes to the other arts, in this case the theatre, for a gesture which is recognisable and somewhat stereotyped

Book II Chapter 14

Parson Adams visits Parson Trulliber. Trulliber is a parson only on Sunday; the other six days he is a farmer. He is especially proud of his fat hogs, which he sells. Learning that Adams is not a customer, Trulliber takes a dislike to him because of his poor appearance. Trulliber is especially concerned that the parson might be travelling on foot and thus lowering the dignity of the clergy. When Adams attempts to borrow money to pay his bill at the inn, he is insulted by Trulliber who will give him nothing. Adams tells him that Christians must be charitable towards others; it is the main command of the Bible. Anyone without charity is no Christian. Trulliber wants to fight Adams, who departs after saying that he is sorry to see that such a person should be a clergyman.

NOTES AND GLOSSARY:

without good works: a central theme of the novel. For Fielding Christianity is expressed through charity towards others and good works, in contrast to those who hold that biblical knowledge and faith are sufficient to salvation

Book II Chapter 15

Adams returns to the inn where he tells the hostess he cannot pay their bill; she surprises Fanny by agreeing to trust Adams. She thinks Adams is the brother of Parson Trulliber, who is a powerful man in the neighbourhood. Adams left his hat and coat at Trulliber's house. The hostess goes to fetch them and learns that Trulliber detests Adams. When she returns she says she will have Joseph, Fanny and Adams arrested if they leave without paying her. No rich person in the neighbourhood will lend Adams the money; but a poor pedlar charitably lends them all he has, which is just enough to pay their bill. They leave the inn, Adams declaring that he will never go there again.

Book II Chapter 16

The three travellers walk about two miles when a gentleman invites them to have beer at the local inn. The gentleman pretends to be pleased with Parson Adams and promises him a future position as his clergyman, horses to take them on their journey and beds at his house for the night. But he keeps giving excuses for his inability to fulfil his promises. After the travellers have stayed the night at the inn, Adams sends the gentleman's messenger to borrow money to pay their bill. The messenger returns to say the gentleman has gone away. The innkeeper says that the man always deceives people with promises. As the innkeeper honours the clergy, he will trust Adams and offers him another pot of beer.

NOTES AND GLOSSARY:

whose heart was naturally disposed to love and affection: those who love others generously and without suspicion are good in contrast to those who are prudent, calculating or vain. Adams is naturally loving towards others

a man of fashion: this chapter continues the satire of the hypocrisies and uncharitable ways of respectable society. The man of fashion is contrasted to the host of the inn

Book II Chapter 17

Adams and his host discuss the squire who has often ruined people by making promises he had no intention of fulfilling. Although Adams is shocked, the host says that as a sailor he learned from his experience of the world never to trust anyone, to which the parson replies that, with the aid of his books, 'I have travelled a great deal farther than you without the assistance of a ship'. Their disagreement over the relative value of book learning and actual experience drifts into an argument concerning the importance of trade and commerce. The host claims that without the necessities and luxuries provided by business and especially by the sailors who make international trade possible, life would be much poorer. Adams claims that trade is based on 'the extravagances of life', while the clergyman's learning fills the soul with holiness and love. The host objects that the clergymen seldom actually do this. Just as a quarrel is about to start, Joseph and Fanny urge Adams to leave and to continue their journey.

Book III Chapter 1

Fielding prefaces Book III with praise of biography, 'the lives of great men', in contrast to writing that confuses romance with history.

Historians may have their facts right but they differ in their interpretations of the characters they describe. Biographers, by which Fielding means novelists, may mistake facts, but show the truth about human nature and general types of character. The novelist should not invent his own materials, but should copy nature. Art should be based on what is generally true to all nations and ages, and not the particulars of one age or country. While good literature is based on real people, it is based on the species, not on individuals; the writer is concerned with manners, not specific men. The manners or types of behaviour that are the concerns of art can be found in all ages. Art satirises general faults with the object of correcting behaviour. Individuals in novels represent a class or type of behaviour; but not every person belonging to a social group or profession is represented by the universal type.

NOTES AND GLOSSARY:

Voltaire: in Letter 18 of *Letters Concerning the English Nation*, Voltaire (1694–1778) uses *Stilts* to describe the figurative language of English tragedy

I describe not men, but manners: the basic eighteenth-century aesthetic position: art should portray universal, timeless types, not individuals

when the first mean selfish creature: Fielding's usual view that selfishness and pride are the cause of bad conduct towards others

distinguishes the satirist from the libeller: satire being general does not insult an individual and therefore aids people to change their behaviour: the classical defence of satire in contrast to the lampoon of an individual (we now tend to confuse the two categories when we speak of satire)

caution more: the description of Fielding's method which follows explains the relationship of his character types to reality. His characters usually are representative of a class of individuals. His art generalises but it is necessary to remember that there are exceptions to each generalisation. To laugh at or satirise a well known fault of a group of people does not mean that everyone in that group is guilty of the conduct described

Book III Chapter 2

After leaving the inn, Joseph, Fanny and Adams travel during a dark, starless night. When Adams sees a light in the distance, he thinks it is a ghost. After hearing voices and the sound of combat, they escape. Joseph carries Fanny down a steep hill. Eventually they are admitted to a house where they are offered refreshment. Some strangers enter. They are sheep thieves whom Adams has mistaken for ghosts. The Master of the House now becomes suspicious of Joseph and Adams and quizzes Adams about Greek. Adams says that he has not read Alexander Pope's translations of Homer's epics. Instead he gives a long, learned discourse on Homer's art and Aristotle's criticism based on his reading in the Greek language. The Master of the House is impressed and asks about Joseph and Fanny. After Adams summarises their recent history, the man offers to tell the story of his own life.

Book III Chapter 3

Born a gentleman and well educated, Mr Wilson was left a 'moderate fortune' by his father. Unwilling to wait until he was twenty-five years old for the money, he successfully contested the will. At seventeen he left school for London in the expectation of making a figure in the world. He obtained good clothes, a wig, and learned to dance, fence and do whatever was necessary to be in fashion. He frequented prostitutes, lived with a courtesan, and as a result needed to be cured of diseases. He had an affair with an older married woman whose husband discovered them, divorced the wife and successfully sued him. Wilson fell in with a group who spent their nights drinking, arguing, over-eating, and gambling, and slept all day. Soon tired of this, he joined a club of free-thinkers who 'threw aside all the prejudices of education' and lived by 'human reason'. At first highly pleased with himself, Wilson became disenchanted when the members of the club were found to act badly. Soon Wilson fell in with gamblers who took what was left of his fortune.

Poverty and distress followed. After trying to earn a living as a writer and as a translator, he was arrested for not paying his debts to his tailor. Although his friends would not help him he was aided by the daughter of a man who had previously swindled him. She was young and beautiful; Wilson married her. They retired into the country and have for twenty years lived a life of 'ease, quiet and love', except that their eldest son was stolen by some gypsies and was never recovered.

NOTES AND GLOSSARY:
penance:	ironic for medical treatment to be cured
whisk:	the card game, whist
eclaircissement:	an understanding, clarification
ignis fatuus:	a will-o'-the-wisp, a false light
on Sundays only:	the law forbade arrests on Sundays except for very serious crimes

club frequented by young men of great abilities: the free-thinkers of the time. Some are Deists and optimistic. Others are moral relativists. Fielding shows that such rational philosophers do not live according to their ideas

Book III Chapter 4

Adams and Wilson have sat up all night drinking and talking. Wilson says he could even now recognise his son by a strawberry mark on his left breast. As the sun rises, they walk in the garden. Wilson and his family provide what they need by gardening. He and his wife, Harriet, are always together and share similar interests. They brew their own drink, including beer, and no longer keep a maidservant as that would breed idleness in their daughters. During breakfast Adams notices the goodwill and charity the family show towards others. By contrast a rich squire's son shouts at the family spaniel, saying he will not allow any dogs in the parish. Adams, Fanny and Joseph leave saying that Wilson lives as people did in the golden age.

NOTES AND GLOSSARY:

That beautiful young lady, the morning: a mock-heroic simile based on the Renaissance practice of comparing a woman rising from her bed to the morning

parterres: level spaces in a garden, occupied by flower-beds

charity: the basic Christian virtue of love. Benevolent kindness towards others is a form of love of God

golden age: according to the ancient Greeks, the first age of man. The Christian equivalent would be Paradise before Adam's fall. Wilson's life in the country, in contrast to his life in the city, offers an ideal marriage and an example of how to live

Book III Chapter 5

Having rested, the trio renew their journey. While walking Joseph and Adams discuss education and schools. Adams believes that public boarding schools are 'the nurseries of all vice and immorality'. Their emphasis is on scholarship, not virtue. Joseph claims that those privately educated at home are often as wicked and, not being part of a society of schoolmates, know nothing about the world. Adams is very strong in his opinion and thinks himself the 'greatest of all schoolmasters'. They stop to have lunch and Adams finds that Mr Wilson has slipped a present of a gold piece among their provisions. Adams praises Wilson's charity and says he will repay him when Wilson visits Adams's parish next week.

NOTES AND GLOSSARY:
whose reward would be great in Heaven: a biblical allusion: 'great is your reward in heaven', Matthew 5:12; 'your reward is great in heaven', Luke 6:23

Book III Chapter 6

Joseph continues speaking of the virtues of charity, which besides doing good brings more honour to the doer than spending wealth to earn a reputation by buying objects. Fanny asks if 'all the great folks' are wicked and is told that there are some exceptions. Adams falls asleep. Joseph and Fanny see a pack of hounds chase and tear to pieces a rabbit. The hounds then bite the sleeping Adams who wakes with a start and runs to escape. The owner of the pack, seeing Adams running, sets his dogs on him. Joseph comes to the rescue. In a passage narrated in a mock-heroic style, Joseph and Adams use their cudgel and stick to stun and wound the vicious dogs. The owner of the pack demands that Joseph stop harming his animals. Joseph replies that he would fight anyone to save Adams. Fanny arrives on the scene and her beauty ends the controversy. The squire invites Adams and Fanny to come to dinner with him.

NOTES AND GLOSSARY:
charity: Fielding's views on proper conduct are summarised by the larger meaning of the word charity. This chapter and the next implicitly contrast the charity of Wilson with the cruelty of the squire. (See the section on 'Charity and good works' on pp.43–5 of these Notes)

at a place called Ross: Alexander Pope praised 'the man of Ross', John Kyrle (1634?–1724), in *Epistle to Bathurst* II, 250–90

it is in the book of verses: Ralph Allen (1693–1764), praised in Alexander Pope's *Epilogue to the Satires*, Dialogue I, 135–6

great *hunter of men*: Nimrod the biblical tyrant, was supposedly a hunter of men. See Genesis 10:9

Life of Cicero: Conyers Middleton's (1683–1750) *The History of the Life of Marcus Tullius Cicero* (1741) was mocked by Fielding in *Shamela*

cudgel: the description is a parody of the shield of Achilles in the *Iliad*, XVIII, 478–613

Amazonian breed: mock-heroic for a bitch; this is an allusion to the Amazons, women warriors

preponderate: to think beforehand

Book III Chapter 7

At the squire's house Joseph and Fanny are sent to eat in the kitchen while Parson Adams eats with the host. The servants are told to make Joseph and the Parson drunk as the squire intends to rape Fanny. The squire is a forty-year-old bachelor who has always been permitted to do what he wishes. He delights in anything eccentric, especially if it is odious to common taste. He especially enjoys making other people appear ridiculous.

At dinner Adams is humiliated in various ways. He loses his temper and accuses his host of inhumanity and lack of charity. The squire says that he would cut Adams's throat if he were not a clergyman. A fake doctor then pretends there was an entertainment which Socrates liked and which they could perform. The scene ends with Adams soaked in a tub of water.

NOTES AND GLOSSARY:

parted from Joseph: the squire thinks Joseph is Parson Adams's servant, and therefore would not invite him to the dining-table

Book III Chapter 8

Adams and Joseph leave the house using their sticks to protect Fanny whom the servants attempt to detain. As soon as the squire hears Fanny has left, he orders his companions to bring her back. Adams and his friends reach an alehouse, called The New Inn, where they eat. After Adams thanks God for the food, a disguised Roman Catholic priest speaks of the folly of worshipping riches. After both clergymen speak at length of their contempt for money, the stranger asks Adams for eighteen pence to pay his bill. Adams searches his pocket for the half-guinea previously given him by Mr Wilson and cannot find it, his pocket having been picked at the squire's house. The priest then leaves, but not before he has persuaded the innkeeper to trust him for future repayment.

NOTES AND GLOSSARY:

our laws: there were severe laws against Roman Catholics. A priest could be accused of high treason for saying mass. Although the extreme laws were seldom enforced, Roman Catholic laymen were often fined and forbidden to practise the professions (law, medicine, and so on)

Rabbit: damn or drat

Book III Chapter 9

In the morning the squire's companions and servants come to the inn. They fight with Joseph and Adams, who resist heroically but are overcome. Fanny is carried off; Joseph and Adams are tied to bed-posts.

NOTES AND GLOSSARY:

hanger: a broad but short sword

huge stone pot ... with both: an imitation of the *Aeneid* XII, 896–902, where Turnus hurls a huge stone at Aeneas, which Virgil claims it would have needed twelve men to lift

with a lumpish noise: mock-heroic version of a recurring phrase in the *Iliad*: 'He fell with a thud, and his armour clanged upon him'

artificial noses are conjoined: venereal disease often attacks the nose and causes its loss

Book III Chapter 10

The action is interrupted for an argument between a poet and a player over the poverty of the theatre of the time. The poet blames actors for ruining the plays; the actor blames the writers for bad plays.

Book III Chapter 11

Joseph regains consciousness and begins to lament the loss of Fanny. Parson Adams tells him that the duty of a Christian is to submit to fate. Joseph claims that is no comfort.

Book III Chapter 12

The Captain warns Fanny that if she does not willingly give her virginity to the squire she will be forced. Two men armed with pistols rescue her and take the Captain prisoner. The horsemen are accompanying a gentleman in a chariot, who turns out to be Peter Pounce, Lady Booby's steward (see Book I, Chapter 10). The chariot, with Fanny and Peter, proceeds to the inn where Adams and Joseph are bound. After they are freed, Peter Pounce offers to take Fanny in his chariot for the remainder of the journey. She refuses, saying she wishes to remain with Joseph. They find Adams's horse and shortly arrive at Booby Hall.

NOTES AND GLOSSARY:

bond and judgment: a certificate in which the debtor's goods are pledged as a security for repayment

come to the parish: under the Poor Law the parish had to take care of those in poverty

---

Book III Chapter 13

Book III ends with a discussion of charity between Parson Adams and Peter Pounce. Adams defines charity as 'a generous disposition to relieve the distressed'. Peter claims that the worst law is that which makes parishes take care of their poor. Peter resents having to pay for charity and claims he is not as well off as he appears. He then insults Adams, who leaves the chariot in anger and joins Joseph and Fanny on their journey to the parish.

Book IV Chapter 1

Lady Booby still dreams of Joseph and makes various excuses for his not loving her. She decides to retire into the country. On her way to Booby Hall, she is surprised to see Joseph. Parson Adams takes Fanny and Joseph to his house. On Sunday Lady Booby is at church when Parson Adams announces the coming marriage of Joseph Andrews and Frances Goodwill. When Lady Booby returns home, she summons Parson Adams.

NOTES AND GLOSSARY:
They flocked about him like dutiful children: Parson Adams is father of his parishioners, like a biblical patriarch
which nothing but benevolence: 'benevolence' brings satisfaction and happiness
I publish the banns ...: the marriage must be announced three times before it can take place, so that objections may be made known

---

Book IV Chapter 2

Lady Booby threatens Parson Adams for befriending Joseph when she has dismissed him from her employ. She commands Adams not to publish the banns again, and thus not allow Joseph and Fanny to have a church marriage. If he does, she will have Adams dismissed from the curacy. 'Then you and the greatest beauty in the parish may go and beg together.' Adams replies that as God is his master, God will provide.

NOTES AND GLOSSARY:
pay for a licence: he has not paid for the licence that would officially allow him to preach

Book IV Chapter 3

Lady Booby sends for Lawyer Scout; she wants to prevent Joseph and Fanny from residing in the parish. When Lawyer Scout explains how he can manipulate the law to prevent Joseph from staying, Lady Booby becomes angry and demands instead that he prevent Fanny from settling there. She claims that Fanny will breed many children who will need charity from the parish. Still angry, she tells Scout to have both Joseph and Fanny removed from the parish. He says that he will have Justice Frolick commit them to prison in London.

NOTES AND GLOSSARY:

hang or transport: a great number of crimes in the eighteenth century were punishable by hanging. Often the death sentence was suspended and the guilty person shipped (transported) to Australia or the American colonies

then he is not removeable: a man could not be removed from a parish if he married

Bridewell: Bridewell Hospital, London, was a house of correction for petty criminals and social undesirables

an act of parliament: in 1729 parliament said that a lawyer had to be qualified to practise. Lawyer Scout was never properly qualified

Book IV Chapter 4

Two days later Lady Booby hears Parson Adams publish the banns again at church. Returning home she meets Slipslop who informs her that Joseph and Fanny have been taken as criminals before Justice Frolick. Slipslop is upset and cries that Joseph will be hanged! Lady Booby wants Fanny removed from the parish but Joseph to remain. While she puzzles on what to do next, a servant announces that her nephew, Mr Booby, and his wife have arrived in a coach. This is the first Lady Booby has heard of her nephew's marriage. She is introduced to his wife, 'that charming Pamela', sister of Joseph.

Book IV Chapter 5

As soon as Mr Booby learns from his servants that Joseph is committed to trial he visits the judge so that his wife's brother may be freed and Pamela and Joseph reunited. When he arrives the judge is in the process of sending Joseph and Fanny to prison in London. Their supposed crime is 'a kind of felonious larcenous thing'. While crossing a field, Joseph broke from a tree a twig that he gave to Fanny. On their way back to Lady Booby's they see Parson Adams; he is invited to join Joseph and Fanny in Squire Booby's coach. The squire now tells Joseph that he has married Pamela. At the house he informs Lady Booby that Joseph is now his brother-in-law and requests that he be admitted to their circle and treated as a gentleman. Lady Booby, secretly still in love with Joseph, immediately agrees 'to entertain him'. But as soon as her nephew mentions Fanny, Lady Booby becomes angry. The squire returns to Joseph and tells him that he must stay with his sister Pamela, while Fanny returns to Parson Adams's house.

Book IV Chapter 6

Lady Booby is disturbed by the tenderness with which Joseph and Pamela embrace each other at their meeting. Parson Adams agrees that Joseph and Fanny can marry on Monday. Lady Booby pretends to have always been superior to love, even with her dead husband. Slipslop, insulted by a remark, protests that servants 'have flesh and blood'. 'Mr Andrews himself is proof that they have as good, if not better,' she says.

NOTES AND GLOSSARY:
as old as the flood: the Deluge in the book of Genesis, at which time
God destroyed most of mankind. Modern families
are supposedly descended from Noah's sons

Book IV Chapter 7

The narrator talks about love. Women are taught by their mothers and later by friends to hate men as monsters. But eventually without realising it they fall in love. So, Lady Booby loved Joseph long before she knew it. Having designs on Joseph she tells her nephew that she will accept the Andrews family, into which he married through Pamela, as her relations. But she wants Joseph not to marry Fanny. Mr Booby attempts to persuade Joseph to break off his planned marriage, but Joseph refuses. Pamela says of Fanny, 'She was my equal', but, 'I am no longer Pamela Andrews'. As the wife of Mr Booby she claims to be 'above' Fanny.

Meanwhile Fanny is walking when a young gentleman approaches her. He attempts to ravish her, but she fights him off. When his servant attempts to rape her, she is saved by Joseph who has come upon the scene.

Book IV Chapter 8

Mrs Adams attempts to persuade her husband not to publish the marriage banns as it would make Lady Booby angry. Joseph and Fanny enter. Adams tells Joseph that he should have patience and wait to marry Fanny in church. He then lectures him concerning the need to accept the ways of Divine Providence. Someone enters and tells the parson that his youngest son has drowned. Adams acts with all the passion and lack of resignation of which he accused Joseph. The son, however, is alive; he fell into a river and was saved by a pedlar. Mrs Adams tells Joseph not to believe her husband; a man should love his wife as much as possible.

NOTES AND GLOSSARY:

submission to superiours: in the eighteenth century it was still expected that the lower classes would obey their social superiors

Abraham so loved his son Isaac: see the Bible, Genesis 22:1–18, where God tests Abraham by demanding Isaac be sacrificed

Book IV Chapter 9

Lady Booby decides to bring Fanny and the Beau together in the hope that his fine appearance will win the girl's love and make her abandon Joseph. Lady Booby and Beau Didapper visit Parson Adams. A description of Beau Didapper follows. He is short, misshapen, effeminate and self-satisfied. Lady Booby shows Fanny to the Beau. Dick is asked to read a story.

NOTES AND GLOSSARY:

so little subject to lust: despite his being attracted to Fanny, there is a strong implication of homosexuality about Beau Didapper

so very large a share: the description of Beau Didapper echoes Conyers Middleton's dedication to John, Lord Hervey (1696–1743) of the *Life of Cicero* (1741). In *Shamela* Fielding parodied Middleton's dedication

Book IV Chapter 10

Dick reads a story about two friends, Leonard and Paul. Leonard becomes rich; Paul becomes a poor soldier. Paul goes to stay at Leonard's estate and overhears many arguments between husband and wife. When Leonard asks for advice, Paul tells him to yield in disputes rather than making them worse. The wife then thinks Paul is 'her friend, and of her side'. Instead he tells her that as a wife she should submit to her husband. The husband and wife ask Paul to referee any differences between them. After any dispute Paul privately tells the husband that he is right, the wife that she is right. Eventually during an argument, the husband and wife cite Paul's opinion and discover his duplicity. They both feel that he has betrayed them and become cold towards him. As a result Paul and Leonard begin to argue.

Book IV Chapter 11

Beau Didapper makes advances towards Fanny. Joseph, angered, hits him. Mr and Mrs Booby disapprove of Joseph's defending Fanny and of his being intent upon marrying a girl of such a class. Haughty Pamela chides Fanny for 'aiming at such a match as her brother'.

NOTES AND GLOSSARY:
satisfaction: promise of a duel
pocket-glass: a small mirror
two children: Adams is their spiritual father. The scene contrasts
                       the Christian love of Joseph, Parson Adams and
                       Dick with the snobbishness, pride and self-interest
                       of the Boobys and Pamela

Book IV Chapter 12

The pedlar tells Fanny that he knows of her parents. A woman he once lived with confessed before she died that years ago she travelled with some gypsies who kidnapped a young girl from the Andrews family and sold her to a Sir Thomas Booby as a servant. Fanny, hearing the story, faints. It appears that Joseph is her brother and Pamela is her sister! Parson Adams gives thanks that the secret has been discovered before incest is committed by Joseph and Fanny.

Book IV Chapter 13

Lady Booby, too lovesick and jealous to eat, takes to her bed and complains to Slipslop, who tells her that Fanny will be removed from Joseph by being kidnapped. Lady Booby laments to herself about her humiliating love for Joseph, a footman. Slipslop returns to tell her that a strange pedlar claims that Fanny and Joseph are sister and brother. Everyone then gathers at Booby Hall to hear the pedlar's story. Mr Booby says that Mr Andrews and his wife will arrive the next morning and will confirm or disprove the story.

NOTES AND GLOSSARY:
virtue and prudence: Fielding is being ironic. Lady Booby's thoughts of 'prudence' here are the result of vanity, not virtue or reason

---

Book IV Chapter 14

Beau Didapper plans to slip into Fanny's bed at night by pretending to be Joseph. He mistakenly enters Slipslop's room. Her cries of alarm bring a naked Parson Adams to the rescue. In the dark he mistakes Slipslop for a man and they fight while Beau Didapper escapes. Lady Booby finds them and assumes the naked parson is attacking Slipslop. She sees the fine clothes the Beau has left, and the situation is explained. Adams starts back to his bedroom, but takes the wrong turn, enters Fanny's room and, naked, falls asleep unknowingly alongside her. When Joseph enters, the parson awakens believing that witchcraft has taken place. At first angry, Joseph knows the parson's eccentricities and understands there has been a mistake.

NOTES AND GLOSSARY:
gallery: the passage or hallway to which the rooms were connected
prudent: the word is used ironically. Fielding believed in natural goodness, benevolence and an open nature. He disliked the contemporary tendency towards prudence as represented, for example, by Richardson's Pamela
As the cat: a comic simile
Assuring Adams: Joseph has matured emotionally since his innocence and inexperience in Book I. He is now understanding and wise, whereas Adams has begun to appear a lovable eccentric who lacks the younger man's sense of judgement

---

Book IV Chapter 15

Mr and Mrs Andrews arrive. Mrs Andrews claims Fanny as her daughter. Mr Andrews went abroad while his wife was pregnant. She gave birth to a daughter who was stolen by gypsies, who left behind a boy. The boy is Joseph, whom Mrs Andrews raised as her own child. The pedlar claims that Joseph was the child of a gentleman, Mr Wilson. Joseph was stolen by gypsies who later, when he was ill, left him with Mrs Andrews when they stole Fanny. Mr Wilson arrives and hearing the story identifies Joseph from a strawberry mark on his breast.

NOTES AND GLOSSARY:

a poor sickly boy: the story of two children exchanged at birth who are then raised without knowing their true parents is the basis of many literary works, since at least the time of the ancient Greeks. Fielding is somewhat humorously using the convention

take care of this poor child: Mrs Andrews practises benevolence. Instead of showing anger she pities the poor child

would perhaps one day restore me: Fanny *is* restored to her at the end of the novel. Perhaps we are to see God's Providence at work in the plot. The good are rewarded

discovery of a stolen child: like the exchange of children, the recognition or discovery scene is an old literary device. There is always a mark, a ring, or some means of identifying the child. Readers would be familiar with this literary convention and would see it as an amusing way of bringing the novel to a happy ending

embracing him: notice here and in the description later in the paragraph when Joseph throws himself at his father's feet that the scene is similar to an eighteenth-century painting. Emotions are externalised into conventional gestures. The effect is supposedly typical of behaviour in such situations. Fielding, with his eighteenth-century Augustan, neo-classical taste, emphasises what is universal

---

Book IV Chapter 16

Joseph obtains his father's permission to marry Fanny. They are wedded by Parson Adams in church. Adams rebukes Mr Booby and Pamela for laughing in church. After the wedding and a feast, 'the happy, the best moment' arrives when Joseph and Fanny 'enjoy the private rewards of their constancy'. Mr Booby gives Fanny two thousand pounds which she and Joseph use to purchase an estate. Soon Fanny will have her first child. Mr Booby offers Mr Adams a position with a better income. Adams refuses to quit his parishioners, but then decides to accept the offer. With the additional money he can hire another curate to help him tend both parishes.

NOTES AND GLOSSARY:

a happy Conclusion: in a comedy, tragedy is averted and the ending is happy. Fielding adheres to the classical formula

Pamela, who behaved with great decency on the occasion: an ironic gibe at Richardson's heroine

rebuked Mr Booby and Pamela: another gibe at Pamela's supposedly virtuous character

done no less to the highest prince: Fielding contrasts the respect due to social superiors with the greater respect due to religion

might keep a curate: Adams faces a conflict. He disapproves of 'pluralism', the common practice of having a position in several parishes, as this results in neglect of duties. But his present salary is so small that he can barely take care of his own family. He compromises by accepting the better-paid position and using part of the new income to appoint another clergyman to help him

High-Life: an allusion to John Kelly's *Pamela's Conduct in High Life* (1741) and to Richardson's continuation of *Pamela*, '*In her EXALTED CONDITION*' (1741)

Part 3

Commentary

The main characters

Parson Abraham Adams

Parson Abraham Adams is a scholar with a perfect knowledge of Greek and Latin and of such modern European languages as French and Italian. He often uses Latin expressions, and during the novel he journeys with a manuscript of Aeschylus's plays in Greek. Brave, friendly and without malice or envy, he is a man of 'good sense' and 'good nature', but 'ignorant of the ways of this world'. He is about fifty years old and has a wife and six children whom he can barely support on his very small income as a curate. Adams enjoys drinking beer. He considers all his parishioners, especially Joseph and Fanny, as his children. He is eccentric and forgetful; he often leaves his hat behind and must return for it.

Joseph Andrews

Joseph Andrews is supposedly the only son of Gaffar and Gammer Andrews and the brother of Pamela. In fact he is the son of Mr Wilson. Joseph was stolen by gypsies as a child and left with Mrs Andrews who brought him up as her own son. Mr Wilson recognises him by a strawberry mark on his breast.

At the early age of ten he is made an apprentice to Sir Thomas Booby and at seventeen becomes Lady Booby's footman. He has a very musical voice, is virtuous and handsome. Well read in the Bible and influenced by Parson Adams, he preserves his purity in the midst of temptations. At the time of the novel he is twenty-one years old. He has nut-brown, curly hair and dark eyes.

Fanny Goodwill

Fanny Goodwill is the child of Mr and Mrs Andrews and the sister of Pamela. She was stolen by gypsies in her infancy. At the age of three she was sold to Sir Thomas Booby and raised as a servant in Lady Booby's family. She is poor, and can neither write nor read. She is very modest, nineteen years old, tall, well shaped but slightly plump, with swelling breasts and large hips, chestnut-brown hair, high forehead and black, sparkling eyes.

Sir Thomas Booby

Sir Thomas Booby is the uncle of Mr John Booby and the husband of Lady Booby. He estimates men 'merely by their dress, or fortune'. He dies early in the novel (Book I, Chapter 5).

Lady Booby

The wife of Sir Thomas Booby, she is a woman 'of gaiety' who thinks the countryside brutish. She takes Joseph to London with her as a servant, attempts to seduce him, and when unsuccessful dismisses him from her service. Later, still desiring him, she tries to prevent his marriage to Fanny. She is very conscious of her social superiority and feels strong conflicts between her passion for Joseph and her humiliation at loving her servant. Besides being extremely interested in men, she often plays cards.

Mrs Slipslop

Mrs Slipslop is a paid companion to Lady Booby. She is of gentle birth, the daughter of a curate. She believes herself to be learned and disputes theology with Adams. She is an 'affecter of hard words' and often mispronounces what she intends to say or uses the wrong words (malapropisms). Forty-five years old, short, heavy-set, red-faced, large-nosed and pimpled, she is not attractive. She falls in love with Joseph and attempts to seduce him. While she also attempts to act as socially superior to him, she admits that Joseph is worth more than most high-born gentlemen.

Pamela Andrews

Pamela Andrews is based on the heroine of Richardson's *Pamela*, who as a servant protects her chastity until her rich employer, Mr B—, failing to seduce her, marries her. In *Joseph Andrews* she is the supposed sister of Joseph, and, unknown to her, the sister of Fanny. Joseph looks upon her as a model of chastity and believes she is engaged to marry a Parson Williams. She is employed by and eventually marries Squire Booby. Now a gentlewoman, she objects to Joseph's marrying Fanny, who, she claims, is a 'social inferior'.

Peter Pounce

Steward to Lady Booby, Peter Pounce grows rich holding back the salaries of the servants and charging them high interest on loans he makes.

Mr Wilson

Mr Wilson is the father of Joseph Andrews. Born in a good family and well educated, Wilson early inherits his father's estate. At the age of seventeen he goes to London, where he follows every fashionable vice, soon wastes his money, attempts to support himself as a writer, becomes destitute and is imprisoned. He is saved from debt by a woman whom he eventually marries and with whom he retires to the country. His eldest son (Joseph) was stolen by some gypsies.

Squire Booby

The nephew of Lady Booby and the husband of Pamela, Squire Booby is based on Mr B— in Richardson's *Pamela*.

Beau Didapper

Beau Didapper is a typical late-seventeenth-century or eighteenth-century dandy who dresses in fashionable clothes, is impertinent to social inferiors, and takes advantage of women. One night he attempts to rape Fanny, but mistakenly enters Mrs Slipslop's room.

The themes of *Joseph Andrews*

Pamela and Joseph Andrews: models of virtue

Richardson's *Pamela: or, Virtue Rewarded* is an epistolary novel in which the story is told through the letters the heroine writes to her parents. Pamela, a chaste servant, fears but is attracted towards her employer, the rich Mr B—. She resists his advances and preserves her virginity until he marries her.

Although Pamela was intended as an example of moral purity, her career could be seen as an example of tough-minded calculation in which sexual virginity is exchanged for marriage and social advancement. The subtitle of Richardson's novel, *Virtue Rewarded*, refers more to the material than the spiritual benefits the heroine derives from her chastity.

Fielding objected to *Pamela*. He thought the epistolary manner of narration long-winded and monotonous and the novel generally tasteless. More significant, Pamela's defence of her chastity until marriage seemed more a strategy to win a rich husband than an example of genuine Christian virtue. Fielding first parodies Richardson's novel in *Shamela*. Where Richardson claimed to be the editor of Pamela's correspondence, Fielding offers what are supposedly the true letters of Shamela. Richardson included with the second edition of *Pamela* a poem and many pages of letters praising his novel; Fielding includes various commendations to himself. Pamela, using the present tense, writes detailed letters about the events in her life; Shamela also, even in bed, writes letters. Scene after scene in *Pamela* is burlesqued—especially the bedroom scenes—to invert Richardson's perspective of his heroine's purity.

Joseph Andrews is not a parody or burlesque of Richardson's *Pamela*, although in places it does mock or satirise Richardson's heroine. Early in Book I Fielding parodies the main situation in *Pamela*—a poor servant remaining sexually chaste when pressed by the advances of a wealthy employer—but such imitation is dropped after Book I, Chapter 10. Pamela herself does not appear as a character in *Joseph Andrews* until Book IV, Chapter 4, after which she remains a minor presence until the novel's conclusion. In Book IV, Pamela is treated less as a figure of fun than as snobbish and cold; she is no different from the hypocrites and pretenders whom Joseph and Adams meet on their journey.

Pamela is first mentioned in Book I, Chapter 1, where Fielding ironically praises 'the excellent essays or letters prefixed to the second and subsequent editions' of Richardson's novel. In Book I, Chapter 3, Joseph, like Pamela, becomes a servant of the wealthy. After Mr B—'s wife dies, Pamela becomes the object of his passions. Lady Booby's attempt to seduce Joseph after the death of her husband parodies Mr B—'s attempts on Pamela (Book I, Chapters 4–9). Joseph, like his sister, defends his virtue. Like Pamela, he is physically aroused, but, unlike his sister (as we learn in Book I, Chapter 11), is saving his chastity for someone else. Similar to Pamela, he writes letters recording his plight (Book I, Chapters 6 and 10). In the first letter Joseph mentions Parson Williams, who, in *Shamela*, Fielding claims was Pamela's lover before she attracted and married Mr B—. By raising this subject again in *Joseph Andrews*, Fielding is again mocking Pamela as a supposed model of virtue. In Book I, Chapter 8 Joseph is shown defending his virginity against Lady Booby. When Lady Booby says 'Did ever mortal hear of a man's virtue', Joseph replies: 'Madam ... that boy is the brother of Pamela, and would be ashamed, that the chastity of his family, which is preserved in her, should be stained in him.' The situation is a reversal of normal social roles, and Joseph is made to appear absurd.

If Joseph's imitation of Pamela's virtue seems comic, our perspective begins to change with Book I, Chapter 11, when we learn of his love for

Fanny, whom he wishes to marry. During the course of the novel we see that Fanny and Joseph are in love and have only been restrained from an early marriage or from indulging their passions by Parson Adams's teachings. They both feel strongly attracted towards each other sexually, but they think that their salvation and eternal life depend upon their conduct. Unlike those who hold that grace and faith are sufficient to salvation, Joseph and Fanny believe, as they have been taught by Adams, in good works and following the Church's teachings.

Are they wrong to deny their passions? The burlesque of Joseph's chastity early in the novel may lead some readers to see this as Fielding's message; but those who indulge their lust are shown to come to an evil end. Even Betty, the good-hearted chambermaid who helps Joseph, suffers from venereal disease and sleeps around indiscriminately. The stories of Wilson and Leonora show some of the consequences of lack of sexual fidelity. While virginity is not in itself virtuous, the correct place for sexuality would appear to be in a faithful marriage where it forms the basis of happiness and love. This is different from Pamela's supposedly calculating attitude towards virginity as a means of being rewarded with a rich husband.

When Pamela does appear personally in *Joseph Andrews*, she is married to Squire Booby. She is tender and warm towards Joseph (Book IV, Chapter 6), but rather jealous of her husband's praise of Fanny. She proudly announces that Fanny 'was my equal' but is now beneath her since her marriage to Squire Booby (Book IV, Chapter 7). Pamela assumes that 'the assistance of grace' will enable her to behave properly, and when she learns that Fanny is her sister, Pamela does behave 'with great decency on the occasion' (Book IV, Chapter 16), a phrase which is used sarcastically by Fielding. At the wedding of Joseph and Fanny, Pamela is rebuked by Parson Adams for laughing in church, which satirises her supposed piety (Book IV, Chapter 16). *Joseph Andrews* ends with Fielding saying that Joseph has retired and will not 'make his appearance in *High-Life*', which is usually understood as a satirical glance at Richardson's continuation of *Pamela*, which shows her happily wedded in high society, '*In her EXALTED CONDITION*' and a book by John Kelly entitled *Pamela's Conduct in High Life*. The satire of Pamela in Book IV of *Joseph Andrews* is concerned with her snobbishness and acceptance of conventional social standards. *Joseph Andrews* illustrates, in the characters of Joseph, Fanny and Adams, what true Christian behaviour should be in contrast to Richardson's model in *Pamela*.

Charity and good works

The three main Christian virtues are faith, hope and charity. Faith guided the Israelites through their journey to the Promised Land; the biblical patriarch Abraham is a model of faith; Parson Abraham Adams has faith in Divine Providence and guides Joseph towards his promised marriage with Fanny and the rewards of a good life lived according to Christian virtues.

Hope is the expectation of something unseen. Christians, for example, have hope of salvation and an eternal after-life. Parson Adams has hope. He continually warns Joseph against giving way to despair. Although he is known to lose control sometimes over his feelings, Adams trusts Divine Providence and expects virtuous behaviour to be rewarded in Heaven.

Charity is love of God and God's creation, in contrast to self-love and the misuse of the creation for personal gain. Charity or love is at the centre of Christian culture. Goodwill, good works, benevolence, kindness and generosity towards others are expressions of charity. *Joseph Andrews* is a demonstration of the reasonableness of benevolence and love. Not only does generosity help others, but those who are charitable are happy, optimistic and find satisfaction from life. Parson Adams preaches goodwill and charitable behaviour; Joseph, under Adams's guidance, practises such conduct.

Many scenes and episodes in the novel are based on contrasts between charity and self-interest or between charity and pretended Christian behaviour. Those who are not charitable are usually hypocrites with pretensions to Christian virtue. Often Fielding builds episodes around such contrasts. The contrasts create the significance of themes which accrue around the various events of the narrative. In Book I, Chapter 12 Joseph is robbed, beaten, stripped of his clothing and left unconscious by some robbers. When the stage-coach comes along the road the passengers do not want to help him. No one offers him any clothing, and a lady passenger objects to allowing a naked man in the coach. The postillion is the only one who is charitable. He gives his coat to Joseph, who is taken to an inn where he is attended by the maid, Betty, who obtains some clothing for him from Mr Tow-wouse, the innkeeper. By way of contrast Mrs Tow-wouse objects to helping Joseph: ' "Common charity, a f—t!" says she, "common charity teaches us to provide for ourselves, and our families; and I and mine won't be ruined by your charity, I assure you." '

In Book II, Chapter 14, finding himself without sufficient money to pay for the night he, Fanny and Joseph have spent at an inn, Parson Adams seeks Parson Trulliber's aid. Trulliber is one of the many clergymen in the novel who are neglectful towards their duties and parishioners. His lack of charity is shown by his manners; he tells his wife to serve Adams their worst ale. When Adams asks to borrow seven shillings, Parson Trulliber threatens to have him punished as a vagabond. Adams says that even if he were not a fellow clergyman, he would still deserve charity from another Christian; at this point Trulliber threatens to fight Adams to prove who is the best Christian! In contrast to Trulliber's lack of charity, a pedlar feels sorry for Adams and lends him the last money he possesses. The narrator comments, 'And thus these poor people, who could not engage the compassion of riches and piety, were at length delivered out of their distress by the charity of a poor pedlar.' Immediately afterwards Adams and his friends once more run up a bill at an inn (Book II, Chapter 16), which they cannot pay. Whereas at the previous inn the hostess threatened to have them arrested and would not allow them to leave without paying, this time the host not only trusts Adams to pay him in the future but offers him further hospitality.

Chastity, love and marriage

Fielding's views on chastity and marriage are likely to be misunderstood by many readers. The humour of the early scenes between Joseph and Lady Booby results from the reversal of sexual roles; a strong, attractive twenty-one-year-old man is the innocent who must reject an older woman's advances. The comedy is intensified by Joseph's language and ideas which are those of a frail young lady protecting her chastity. Our perspective on Joseph's chastity changes once we know he is in love with Fanny whom he has promised to marry. The novel implies that sexuality should be an expression of love and that virginity should be preserved until marriage. Parson Adams's insistence that Fanny and Joseph fulfil Church law on marriage results in their being happily married.

Joseph withholds himself from women he does not love because such sexuality would be misuse of love and abuse of his love for Fanny. The evil and vain characters in the novel try to use others for their own benefit; in the realm of sexual activity they attempt to obtain others through tricks, seduction or rape. The many attempted rapes in the novel stand in contrast to the love and fidelity of Joseph and Fanny for each other.

In the novel sexuality outside marriage often results in disease, unwanted children, exploitation, or broken engagements. Mr Wilson's sexual experience as a man about town is unsatisfactory, but his faithful marriage is happy. Betty is likable as she is charitable towards others; but through her early sexual experience she became diseased and she later seeks sexual pleasure without discrimination.

Faith and grace

Within the novel those who believe in salvation through charity and good works are contrasted to those who trust in salvation through faith or grace. The former feel that they must work in this world for their reward in Heaven; the latter expect that because of their belief or because of God's foreknowledge of their goodness they will be saved.

In Book I, Chapter 17, Parson Adams praises Whitfield for wanting to reform the clergy of the Church of England of its 'luxury and splendour'. But Adams turns against Whitfield when the latter 'set up the detestable doctrine of faith against good works':

> one would think none but the Devil himself could have the confidence to preach it. For can any thing be more derogatory to the honour of God, than for men to imagine that the all-wise Being will hereafter say to the good and virtuous, *Notwithstanding the purity of thy life, notwithstanding that constant rule of virtue and goodness in which you walked upon earth, still as thou did'st not believe every thing in the true orthodox manner, thy want of faith shall condemn thee?* Or on the other side, can any doctrine have a more pernicious influence on society than a persuasion, that it will be a good plea for the villain at the last day; *Lord, it is true I never obeyed one of thy commandments, yet punish me not, for I believe them all?*

Adams thinks that 'a virtuous and good Turk, or heathen, are more acceptable in the sight of their Creator, than a vicious and wicked Christian, tho' his faith was as perfectly orthodox as St Paul's himself'. Parson Trulliber is an example of the ill effects of faith without works. He neglects his duties as a clergyman, is uncharitable towards Parson Adams, and orders the latter out of the house when he says that faith without good works will not bring salvation: '"Doest thou speak against faith in my house? Get out of my doors, I will no longer remain under the same roof with a wretch who speaks wantonly of faith and the scriptures."'

Adams replies that if a person really believes in the Bible then he must be charitable. Charity is the main duty expressed in the Bible. (See the section on 'Charity and good works' on pp.43–5 of these Notes.)

Form and style of *Joseph Andrews*

The narrator

The narrator, or teller of a story, may be different from the author. The narrator of *Joseph Andrews* has a distinct character and presence; he holds opinions, comments upon events, and generally may be said to guide the reader through the novel by establishing contact between the author's values and the response of the reader to the story. In Book I, Chapter 1, the narrator uses long, balanced sentences of the kind usually identified with eighteenth-century conservatism:

It is a trite, but true observation, that examples work more forcibly on the mind than precepts: and if this be just in what is obvious and blameable, it is more strongly so in what is amiable and praise-worthy.

The narrator is the voice of common sense and universally held opinions.

But the narrator is also often ironic, satirically meaning the opposite of what he explicitly says:

The reader, I believe, already conjectures, I mean, the lives of Mr Colley Cibber, and of Mrs Pamela Andrews. How artfully doth the former, by insinuating that he *escaped* being promoted to the highest stations in church and state, teach us a contempt of worldly grandeur! how strongly doth he inculcate an absolute submission to our superiors! Lastly, how completely doth he arm us against so uneasy, so wretched a passion as the fear of shame; how clearly doth he expose the emptiness and vanity of that fantom, reputation.

Because the narrator shifts rapidly into irony, the reader is uncertain, even insecure, about how to respond to various statements. We must always be alert for the narrator's irony and sense of humour.

The preface

The establishing of a relationship between narrator and reader in a preface to prose fiction was already a literary convention before *Joseph Andrews*. Cervantes's *Don Quixote* begins with a prologue. Roger Boyle's prose romance *Parthenissa* (1665), William Congreve's *Incognita* (1692) and Daniel Defoe's novel *Colonel Jack* (1722) have prefaces.

The preface to *Joseph Andrews* attempts to explain the nature of the new genre of the novel, in contrast to earlier kinds of prose fiction, and its relationship to the recognised genres of European literature as first defined by Aristotle. Fielding was conscious that *Joseph Andrews* was a new direction for the English novel. The preface offers a theory for the kind of fiction he has written. He distinguishes it from 'romance', by which he means the fantastic heroic and pastoral stories, filled with refined lovers, noble knights, flying horses, magical swords and conquests of foreign nations that were then the most popular kind of fiction. Using the classical Greek division of literature into kinds, he calls his novel a comic epic or comic romance in prose. (During the sixteenth and seventeenth centuries the long romance in verse was sometimes confused with epic poetry.) Similar to the epic, it is large, comprehensive, and contains many incidents and characters. Unlike the serious epic or epic romance (which treat of great persons), it treats of 'persons of inferiour rank' and manner (the *generic* subject matter of comedy) instead of kings and nobles, and it portrays the 'ridiculous'. Instead of a high diction, it sometimes uses burlesque; instead of dignity it is sometimes ludicrous. But Fielding's comic epic does not aim at burlesque, mere buffoonery or clowning, or other kinds of crude comedy, although they may be used on occasion. Rather he aims at portraying what he calls the ridiculous. The ridiculous results from such affectations as vanity and hypocrisy. Pride and falseness are comic because of the discrepancy between what a person does and what he tries to appear. The revelation of such pretences makes the reader aware of the ridiculous.

Universal character types

Eighteenth-century literature aims at portraying what is timeless and universal. Fielding says he describes 'not an individual, but a species' (Book III, Chapter 1). 'The lawyer is not only alive, but hath been so these 4000 years.' Fielding's novels have a conscious artificiality. He does not try to paint a raw slice of life; the life shown is stylised, and makes use of the reader's knowledge of what are common kinds of conduct and social types. 'I describe not men, but manners.' Fielding's characters, therefore, sometimes behave or are described as acting in what appears to us as an artificial, exaggerated fashion. Fielding controls the portrayal of the emotion so that the effect of the feelings is of less importance than our recognition of their universality.

The Manner of Cervantes

The subtitle of *Joseph Andrews* says the book is 'Written in Imitation of The *Manner* of Cervantes, Author of *Don Quixote*'. *Don Quixote* (1605) was transitional in the development of the modern novel from the older fantastic romances of chivalric and heroic behaviour. The story of Cervantes's eccentric knight's journey through a real Spain in search of romantic adventures is perhaps the first comic-epic in prose, or novel, of modern Europe. The absurdity of Don Quixote's misinterpretation of what in fact is low reality for situations in chivalric literature is funny and yet strangely ennobling. Don Quixote's eccentric idealism is highly sympathetic; the knight is a hero of the imagination.

Ways in which *Joseph Andrews* imitates *Don Quixote* are as follows:
(1) The journey of Adams and Joseph through the countryside is like the journey of Don Quixote and Sancho Panza through the country.
(2) The eccentric, idealistic Parson Adams is somewhat like the eccentric, idealistic Quixote; if both are amusing, they are also superior to the less noble-minded, less generous characters whom they meet on their journeys.

(3) The society shown in both books is hypocritical, scheming and proud.

(4) Such technical features as the chapter headings and the digressions within the main story are similar in the two books.

(5) Several incidents occur in both novels. There is also a similarity in concept. In *Fielding's Art of Fiction* (1961), Maurice Johnson says:

> Like Quixote, who was absorbed in a vanished world of chivalry, Abraham Adams amusingly tries to live by the idealistic tenets of Christianity and the Greek and Roman moralists; like Quixote he fearlessly and thanklessly champions the oppressed and weak; like Quixote he is 'as entirely ignorant of the ways of this World as an Infant'.

Another similarity is in the structure and movement of both *Don Quixote* and *Joseph Andrews*. *Don Quixote* begins by apparently burlesquing the chivalric romance. Our first reaction to the eccentric knight is amusement. From Chapter 6 onwards *Don Quixote* becomes less a burlesque than a serious, although humorous book about people in society. What starts as a comic parody of romantic clichés turns into an ironic treatment of the real world. *Joseph Andrews* follows a similar structural pattern. Its opening chapters parody Richardson's idealisation of Pamela's chastity; by making Joseph a strong, vigorous male who protects his virginity against the temptations of older women, Fielding burlesques the equation of virtue with chastity. But after Joseph is dismissed from Lady Booby's service and his journey begins, we are told of his love for Fanny. From this chapter (Book I, Chapter 11) onwards, Joseph begins to develop into a sympathetic character whose warm-blooded idealism is, by the end of the novel, found to be superior both to the calculating chastity of Pamela and to the self-interested 'realism' of those he and Adams meet on their journey. Both Joseph and Parson Adams illustrate that what the world considers foolish, quixotic behaviour is often more sane that hard-headed, supposedly practical conduct.

Burlesque and the mock-heroic

The mock-heroic was a favourite style of late-seventeenth and early-eighteenth century satiric writing. John Dryden's *MacFlecknoe* and Alexander Pope's *The Rape of the Lock* are among the many well known literary works of the period that use an elevated style ironically to make comedy out of contemporary subject matter.

The mock-heroic assumes the reader's familiarity with the diction, conventions and situations of classical literature, especially of the Greek and Roman epics, the epic-romances of the Renaissance, and Milton's

Paradise Lost. In his preface Fielding says that his comic romance may include some burlesque, burlesque imitations and parodies. 'But tho' we have sometimes admitted this in our diction, we have carefully excluded it from our sentiments and characters.' Fielding distinguishes between works which in passages contain mock-heroic touches and works which are consistently mock-heroic. His novel is comic but not mock-heroic, whereas some literary works of the period consistently written in an inflated style have the effect of deflating or mocking their subject by the implied contrast between the high diction and the low or realistic life portrayed. Fielding's purpose is to entertain the reader through humour, whereas the mock-heroic style is normally used to satirise or burlesque its subject matter.

While a knowledge of classical literature—which was part of the education of most eighteenth-century readers—adds to the appreciation of Fielding's mock-heroic touches, such learning is not necessary. Usually the discrepancy between what is being said and the manner or style of telling will seem humorous to the reader whether or not he is aware of which heroic conventions are being imitated and parodied.

Some examples of the mock-heroic may be useful. It is common in the epic, romances and other grand narrative forms to list the family lineage of the hero and main characters. The persons and events of the work are given nobility by showing that the heroes and warriors are descended from gods, famous kings and other grand ancestors. The convention of listing the hero's ancestors is imitated in Book I, Chapter 2, but the result is a comic anti-climax. After beginning grandly with 'the hero of our ensuing history', 'brother to the illustrious Pamela', Joseph Andrews's only notable ancestor was a great grandfather who 'was an excellent cudgel-player'. But if Joseph has no well known family history, 'it is sufficiently certain, that he had as many ancestors, as the best man living'. After an elevated or neutral-sounding beginning, Fielding's sentences often end in a comic anti-climax.

Besides parodying epic conventions, Fielding often uses heroic similes:

> As when a hungry tygress, who long had traversed the woods in fruitless search, sees within the reach of her claws a lamb, she prepares to leap on her prey; or as a voracious pike of immense size, surveys through the liquid element a roach or gudgeon which cannot escape her jaws, opens them wide to swallow the little fish: so did Mrs Slipslop prepare to lay her violent amorous hands on the poor Joseph.

Epic poetry often contains 'sentences', high-sounding general observations. In the following example, the insertion of 'whose name I have forgot' deflates the impressive sounding sentence: 'It is the observation of some antient Sage, whose name I have forgot, that passions operate differently on the human mind.' Fielding is not satirising the idea contained within the observation; rather he provides some entertaining comedy within the telling of the story. The mock-heroic is used by Fielding in battle scenes where the elevated or epic diction contrasts with the crude violence of the fighting.

The art of variety

Joseph Andrews gives the appearance of casualness. The narrator is relaxed, friendly, comfortable, often comical, and quickly changes the direction of what he is saying. The story itself appears somewhat arbitrary with its various coincidences, its episodes which begin in the middle of one chapter and develop over succeeding chapters, its digressions and interpolated tales, and the way characters appear, disappear and then reappear as various strands of the story are dropped and then later pursued. Fielding has consciously created a work which *appears* to lack economy and order. One purpose of such a feeling of abundance is to give the reader variety; the novel is packed with life, and life itself often seems disorderly and filled with surprises and coincidences. The variety of *Joseph Andrews* is thus an imitation of reality. It is, however, a stylised imitation of reality. Each age has its own notions of what is realistic. For the seventeenth and eighteenth centuries, Fielding's characters seemed typical of kinds of human behaviour, and the events in his novel seemed representative of real life. A nineteenth-century or twentieth-century novel with its close focus on nuances of social behaviour or on individual psychology is likely to seem more realistic to us than Fielding's fiction; but the modern novel usually lacks Fielding's abundance, fullness and variety.

Fielding could write a comic-epic in prose based on coincidences, surprises and a variety of incidents because previous centuries enjoyed complex, surprising tales. Fielding explains what he is doing in *Joseph Andrews*. His preface says it is a 'comic-epic poem in prose'; being an epic its action is 'extended', 'comprehensive' and it contains many 'incidents' and a great 'variety of characters'.

At the beginning of Book II, Chapter 1, Fielding again points to his art of fiction. Although he is speaking in a humorous fashion, his observations reveal the artistic ideas behind the appearance of casualness: 'for first, those little spaces between our chapters may be looked upon as an inn or resting-place, where he may stop and take a glass, or any other refreshment, as it pleases him.' Fielding advises the reader not to:

travel through these pages too fast: for if he doth, he may probably miss the seeing some curious productions of nature which will be observed by the slower and more accurate reader. A volume without any such places of rest resembles the opening of wilds or seas, which tires the eye and fatigues the spirit when entered upon.

The summary of contents before each chapter informs 'the reader what entertainment he is to expect'.

Joseph Andrews is meant to be both morally instructive and entertaining. Renaissance and eighteenth-century artistic theory claimed that education and entertainment must be combined in the same work. The entertainment is provided by the narrative, especially in its variety, surprises and humour.

Digressions

Renaissance and eighteenth-century literature sometimes surprises the modern reader by the inclusion of long digressions which seem unrelated to the main story. Such digressions or interpolated material were considered a pleasant change of pace, or as adding variety to the story. Besides the entertainment that such stories offer—an entertainment sometimes not appreciated by the modern reader trained in the economy, detail and intensity of naturalistic writing—such digressive material was expected to be related to the main story by theme, moral, symbolism, or some ironic inverse relationship. The Renaissance epic uses sub-plots and digressions as reflections of the main plot.

Being a comic-epic, *Joseph Andrews* continues the Renaissance tradition of using digressions as mirrors and indirect commentary on the main narrative. The main digressions are the 'History of Leonora' (Book II, Chapters 4 and 6), Wilson's tale (Book III, Chapter 3) and the story of Leonard and Paul (Book IV, Chapter 10). Leonora is a jilt; her unfaithfulness and subsequent unhappy life is a mirror image of the constancy of Joseph and Fanny. In miniature, it is a contrasting reversal of the main story. Whereas Fanny remains faithful despite Joseph's having gone to London, Leonora soon falls in love with Bellarmine during Horatio's absence. Fanny remains chaste until her marriage; Leonora becomes Bellarmine's mistress. Joseph appears poor but is discovered to be the son of a rich man. Bellarmine seems wealthy, but in fact is using his extravagantly fashionable appearance as a means of obtaining a rich wife. Joseph and Fanny retire to a happy marriage; Leonora, rejected by society, lives alone unhappily. Leonora's story is a warning against trusting appearances, against following fashions, against pre-marital sexuality and against infidelity. She has fallen into the temptations that Joseph and Fanny have resisted. (The relationship of Mr Wilson's tale to the main plot will be discussed in Part 4, under 'Sample questions and answers'. See pp.66–7.)

Fielding's craft

The discovery of Joseph's true parentage is prepared early in the novel. The narrator (Book I, Chapter 2) introduces Joseph by saying he 'was esteemed to be' the only son of Mr and Mrs Andrews. Later Mr Wilson says, 'Within three years of my arrival here I lost my eldest son ... he was stolen away from my door by some wicked travelling people whom they call *Gypsies*; nor could I ever with the most diligent search recover him' (Book III, Chapter 3). The significance of these remarks is revealed when the pedlar begins to unravel the mystery of Joseph's true parentage (Book IV, Chapter 15).

Besides quietly planting throughout the novel necessary information for the conclusion of the story, Fielding also prepares the ground for later themes and incidents. Parson Adams speaks at length to Joseph on the necessity of exercising patience and submission when faced by misfortune (Book III, Chapter 11). While Joseph laments that Fanny has been kidnapped and fears that she will be violated, Adams tells him that it is a Christian's duty to submit to fate, that no one can understand the ways of Divine Providence, that the wise men and philosophers have always taught the folly of grief. Adams again lectures Joseph: 'All passions are criminal in their excess, and even love itself, if it is not subservient to our duty, may render us blind to it' (Book IV, Chapter 8). As an example of submitting to Providence he speaks of Abraham, who accepted God's command to sacrifice Isaac, his son. Warning Joseph not to place all his affections on Fanny, Adams says:

> Now believe me, no Christian ought so to set his heart on any person or thing in this world, but that whenever it shall be required or taken from him in any manner by divine Providence, he may be able, peaceably, quietly, and contentedly to resign it.

He no sooner finishes the sentence than someone rushes in to say that Adams's youngest son has drowned. Adams is immediately thrown into agony. When Joseph attempts to comfort him, Adams exclaims: 'do not go about impossibilities. Had it been any other of my children I could have born it with patience.'

Structure and parallels

The careful organisation of the novel is shown in its structure. The story begins (Book I, Chapter 2) with the supposed history of Joseph's parentage and its penultimate chapter (Book IV, Chapter 15) reveals his true father. The story also begins in the country house of the Boobys (Book I, Chapter 2) which is also in Adams's parish. Joseph, Adams, Lady Booby and Mrs Slipslop, four of the five principal characters, are introduced. (Fanny is not mentioned until Book I, Chapter 11; her late appearance is meant as a surprise.) Immediately the action shifts to London (Book I, Chapter 4). From Book I, Chapter 11 the narrative moves through the countryside as Joseph and later others return towards the parish from which the story began. The overall effect of the novel is to begin with a group of characters who are then dispersed; gradually they come together again and other significant characters are added. Finally the original group, enlarged by Pamela and her husband, Mr Wilson, the pedlar, and Mr and Mrs Andrews, are reassembled for the wedding of Joseph and Fanny.

Douglas Brooks has shown that Fielding took surprising care to provide symmetries within the narrative. In Book IV, for example, Lady Booby reappears and expresses similar passions and conflicting emotions to those expressed in Book I. She even has similar conversations with Mrs Slipslop concerning Joseph in Book I, Chapter 7, and Book IV, Chapter 6. Pamela is mentioned early in Book I and appears towards the end of Book IV. More precise examples of symmetry include the reunions of Joseph and Fanny at inns (Book II, Chapter 12; Book III, Chapter 12); and the attempted rape and abduction of Fanny (Book II, Chapter 9; Book III, Chapter 9).

Besides symmetry and parallels *Joseph Andrews* includes many contrasts which are mirror reversals. Lady Booby's inconstancy (she is unfaithful to her husband, desires Joseph and takes up with 'a young captain of dragoons') is the opposite of Joseph's faithfulness to Fanny. Adams's conduct as a clergyman is contrasted to the behaviour of Parsons Barnabas and Trulliber. Besides these large general contrasts, there are often explicit contrasts within each chapter. In Book II, Chapter 9, a gentleman speaks at length about bravery. He informs Adams that he has disinherited a nephew because he thought him a coward. They then hear some cries. The gentleman, although armed with a gun, hastens away: 'Do you consider this gun is only charged with shot, and that the robbers are most probably furnished with pistols loaded with bullets? This is no business of ours; let us make as much haste as possible out of the way, or we may fall into their hands ourselves.' By contrast Adams, armed only with his crabstick, goes directly towards the sounds and after a battle saves Fanny from being ravished.

Theatrical gestures

In many places in *Joseph Andrews*, especially during scenes of extreme emotion, characters are shown as behaving in a theatrical or stereotyped manner. The gestures are indeed theatrical and stereotyped and are meant to be so.

As the modern novel is naturalistic and aims at reproducing an equivalent feeling to that experienced by the main characters, we expect individual emotion to be reflected in the texture and movement of the prose style. One of Richardson's contributions to the development of the modern novel is to make the reader feel, emotionally participate in, Pamela's anxieties, fears and confusions. Fielding would consider such introspection and lack of perspective to be morbid, tasteless, and running contrary to common sense. If, as Fielding believed, people are types found throughout the ages, and the situations faced by people in all ages are the same, then the focus on individuality in *Pamela* or in Cibber's *Apology* makes these feelings examples of egotism and self-interest, which threaten the accepted traditional values of Christian culture and society.

By contrast, traditional gestures to express emotion are easily recognised and are based on such generally accepted human emotions as love, fear, anger, hate and surprise, which all societies and ages have known. Such conventional gestures also have the effect of holding the reader at a distance from the emotion, thus keeping the event in perspective. If a close focus on emotions intensely involves the reader, distance and stereotyped gestures keep a public view of events. To judge people, to have a sense of humour, to have a comprehensive view of life and to show the workings of Divine Providence, it is useful to be detached, objective and clear-eyed.

There are, however, two other reasons for stereotyped gestures and stylised characterisation:
(1) Fielding was originally a dramatist and seventeenth-century and eighteenth-century theatre made use of conventionalised gestures to express emotion.
(2) The arts in the early eighteenth century were closely aligned, as is shown by Fielding's defence of his practice as similar to Hogarth's style of caricature. Painting, drama, poetry and the novel were among the arts which assumed there existed a widely accepted language of gesture and symbol. The gestures, poses and images taught to actors were used in the other arts.

Because these gestures were well known and widely accepted, a sophisticated writer would often use them somewhat humorously. Such humour did not mean that the writer was burlesquing the scene (treating it as farce), but was an added perspective, a way of keeping the emotion stylised, distant and within the realms of judgement. The conflicting emotions Lady Booby feels for Joseph, Joseph's lamentation over the abduction of Fanny and the various mock-heroic battles are examples of stylised comic or ironic scenes.

Joseph Andrews and the picaresque novel

Joseph Andrews is sometimes called a picaresque novel. The picaresque novel was popular during the sixteenth and seventeenth centuries and told of the various adventures of someone, such as an orphan or criminal, on the fringes of conventional society, during his travels. The *picaro* was a kind of vagabond or adventurer whose journey took him through a wide variety of kinds of life, especially low life, before he was rewarded with riches or happiness. Although few modern novels are, strictly speaking, picaresque novels, many works of fiction are indebted in a general way to the picaresque tradition. Often the hero has no established place in society, is of unknown or poor parentage, travels, has unexpected adventures, and is eventually assimilated into society through marriage, the acquisition of wealth or high status in the community. It is sometimes claimed that the Renaissance saw the picaresque tale as involving a moral journey towards salvation during which the main character was tempted, tested, developed virtue, and then rewarded. *Joseph Andrews* follows this pattern.

The growth of a hero

The epic hero was a warrior, a man of unusual cunning and strength, whose life was intertwined with the destiny of his people. Christian writers of epics were faced with the problem of how to transform the pagan model of a hero into a Christian pattern of virtue. Often, as in Ariosto's *Orlando Furioso* (1515) or Tasso's *Jerusalem Delivered* (1575), the writer made the warrior hero a defender of Christian against non-Christian causes, and showed development in the hero's behaviour from an initial personal anger to a later adjustment to more virtuous behaviour. In *Paradise Lost* (1667) Milton solved the problem of the hero by making Jesus Christ the hero of the poem. In Fielding's comic epic, two good men, Joseph Andrews and Parson Adams, are the heroes. It is their goodness, their charity and benevolence, which makes them moral heroes. Both Andrews and Adams are personally chaste and are charitable towards others.

Is Joseph a hero? Early in the novel his chastity appears comic. Whether or not readers believe in male chastity we laugh at Joseph's discomfort and awkwardness while resisting the advances of Lady Booby. While our view of Joseph is favourably modified when we are told of his love for Fanny, he seems an unlikely hero early in the novel. By contrast the eccentric Parson Adams becomes the main character for many chapters after he discovers Joseph ill at the inn (Book I, Chapter 14). But in the course of the journey to Booby Hall the relationship between Joseph and Adams changes. Through experience of the world

Joseph develops, matures and becomes impressive, whereas Adams is sometimes unable to live up to his own ideals of conduct.

Early in Book IV Adams admirably defies Lady Booby; despite the threat to his job he will publish the banns of marriage between Joseph and Fanny. Joseph defies Mr Booby by saying he will marry Fanny regardless of objections to her low social standing. Shortly afterwards, he saves Fanny from being ravished by a servant of Beau Didapper. During the struggle Joseph is bloodied. Adams preaches to Joseph on the need to accept fate with resignation, but himself gives way to extreme passion when he mistakenly believes his son has drowned. Afterwards when Joseph asks whether his emotions for Fanny are not as valid as those of Adams for his son, the Parson answers, 'such love is foolishness ... it savours too much of the flesh'. He claims men should love their wives with 'moderation and discretion'. Mrs Adams puts an end to the discussion with:

> Fine doctrine indeed! A wife hath a right to insist on her husband's loving her as much as ever he can: and he is a sinful villain who doth not. Doth he not promise to love her, and to comfort her, and to cherish her, and all that? ... Besides, I am certain you do not preach as you practise; for you have been a loving and a cherishing husband to me, that's the truth on't; and why you should endeavour to put such wicked nonsense into this young man's head, I cannot devise. Don't hearken to him, Mr Joseph, be as good a husband as you are able, and love your wife with all your body and soul too.

In this chapter Parson Adams is an example of the ridiculous; he preaches extreme doctrines that in private life he does not practise. Whereas the grotesque hypocrites in the novel speak nobly but act ignobly, Adams is sometimes a hypocrite in preaching a rigid doctrine that he does not feel and that contrasts radically with the generosity, good-heartedness and charity of his character.

A few chapters later Joseph boxes Beau Didapper's ears for insulting Fanny; this is followed by the night of confusion when Parson Adams fights with Mrs Slipslop and is forgiven by Joseph for having mistakenly slept in Fanny's bed. The effect of the various incidents in Books III and IV is to make Adams appear increasingly comic and to make Joseph appear someone of authority, strength and judgement. While it would not be correct to say that Joseph is exalted at the expense of Adams in Book IV, their relative stature in the novel has changed. At the conclusion we are told that Joseph retires to an estate in the country and 'remains blest with his Fanny', while Adams surprisingly makes the practical compromise of accepting a higher paid Church position which allows him to hire a curate to do part of his duties, a practice of which he formerly disapproved.

Biblical allusions and parallels

Since Fielding's intent is to show Christian virtues in the secular world, he uses biblical allusions and parallels in the novel. For an eighteenth-century English reader familiar with the Bible, the references would be instantly recognisable.

An obvious parallel to the Bible occurs in Book I, Chapter 12, after Joseph has been robbed and severely beaten. Those comfortably seated in the stage-coach find various objections to helping him. Of those present it is the postillion, who is socially and economically inferior to the others, who strips off his coat to lend to Joseph so that he can enter the coach without his nakedness offending a lady. The analogy is to the Good Samaritan (Luke 10:30–7), Jesus's parable about the traveller who was stripped of his clothes and wounded by thieves. Various supposedly religious Jews ignore the wounded man who is finally helped by, surprisingly, a Samaritan. The analogy is continued in the next chapter (Book I, Chapter 13), where at the inn to which Joseph is taken only Betty, the chambermaid, helps him, in contrast to Mrs Tow-wouse and the good-natured but uncourageous Mr Tow-wouse.

In Book IV, Chapter 8, there is an ironic use of Genesis 22:1–18. Adams has reminded Joseph that Abraham's faith in God required him to accept the divine command that his son Isaac be a sacrifice. Immediately afterwards a messenger announces that Adams's son has drowned. Instead of accepting fate Parson Adams begins to lament. Just, however, as God saves Isaac, so Dick is found not to be drowned. The irony is that the biblical story is meant to be an example of faith, while Parson Adams, being less perfect than the patriarch Abraham, has understandably given way to human emotions.

The names of the major characters are biblical. Joseph's life and character recall the biblical Joseph, especially in his chastity when faced by sexual advances (see Genesis 39:7–20). The name Abraham Adams combines Adam, the first man of Genesis, with Abraham, a biblical patriarch and a model of faith.

Parallels to Homer's *Odyssey*

Joseph Andrews is a 'comic Epic-poem in Prose'. The eighteenth century often made use of parallels between epic material and contemporary events for various purposes, including dignifying and satirising, or simply because such allusions had become part of the literary technique of the period. The journey of Adams and Joseph may be seen as somewhat like the great voyages depicted in the epics of Homer and Virgil. Some specific parallels, mentioned in Douglas Brooks's edition of *Joseph Andrews*, include the following. Lady Booby's fruitless love of

Joseph parallels Calypso's love of Odysseus. Adams visits the pig-keeper Trulliber (Book II, Chapter 14), a parallel to Odysseus's visit to the swineherd in the *Odyssey*. The parallels to the *Odyssey* are used intermittently. The novel does not offer a sustained parallel or an allegory. Rather Fielding draws upon the educated eighteenth-century reader's knowledge of traditional Western culture to suggest occasional comparisons.

The choice of Hercules

A theme from classical mythology often found in seventeenth- and eighteenth-century literature is the 'choice of Hercules'. According to legend Hercules while at a crossroad is faced by two women, representative of pleasure and virtue. If he chooses the former he will live luxuriously; he chooses the latter and leads a life of virtuous activity. Several times in the novel Fielding suggests a similarity between Joseph and Hercules. Like Hercules as a boy, Joseph 'gave proofs of strength and agility beyond his years' (Book I, Chapter 2). In the description of his physique, there is a similarity to a classical or Renaissance statue of Hercules: 'His legs and thighs were formed in the exactest proportion. His shoulders were broad and brawny, but yet his arms hung so easily, that he had all the symptoms of strength without the least clumsiness' (Book I, Chapter 8). Slipslop will not defend Joseph because she 'would not venture her place for any Adonis or Hercules' (Book I, Chapter 7). Joseph, like Hercules, chooses virtue (Fanny) instead of vice (Lady Booby).

Eighteenth-century contexts

Joseph Andrews is a mirror of early eighteenth-century society and culture. The condition of the clergy, the rise of Methodism, the corruption of politics, new movements in art, the following of French fashions, and the social prominence of the newly rich and of money-lenders are among the contemporary topics to which the novel alludes.

The clergy

After the Restoration of Charles II (1660) and throughout part of the eighteenth century, churchmen were often looked upon with disdain. The lower clergy of the era were poorly paid and badly educated. As there was a surplus of candidates for the few livings available, the parson was dependent upon those with influence for his position and was treated by the nobility as a personal servant. The higher clergy were notoriously worldly, ambitious, proud and felt to be idle and corrupt. It was common for such clergymen to hold more than one appointment and consequently often to be absent from the parish. They left their parishes to poorly paid curates who could not afford books or decent clothes, and were felt to be ignorant, incompetent and servile towards the rich upon whom they were dependent. Such a situation, in which the clergy were either fashionably worldly or humiliated by poverty, undermined respect for religion.

One theme of *Joseph Andrews* is the condition of the clergy at the time. There are seven members of the priesthood in the novel. Barnabas is vain, corrupt, ignorant and a heavy drinker. He is against the literal interpretation of scripture and against reforms of the Church that would make the higher clergy live in a less worldly manner (Book I, Chapter 17). Trulliber is 'a Parson on Sundays' and neglects his parishioners the rest of the week. Uncharitable, proud, hypocritical, he uses his wealth and pretence of gravity to put the parish in fear. Other clergy include the parson who pretentiously and ignorantly mistakes Adams's manuscript of Aeschylus for 'a Manuscript of one of the Fathers' (Book II, Chapter 11); the parson of Adams's parish who carries on a foolish quarrel with Sir Thomas over a small sum of money and who takes pleasure in his law suit, having 'utterly undone many of the poor tenants' (Book I, Chapter 3). We also learn of the proud parson who ignores his parishioners unless they are rich (Book II, Chapter 16).

In contrast to such pride, ignorance, hypocrisy and worldly ambition, Parson Adams is used to illustrate the humiliation suffered by the poverty-stricken lower clergy, and what a true clergyman should be. He loses one curacy when he refuses to accept the rector's demand that he use his influence in an election (Book II, Chapter 8).

The Latitudinarians and benevolence

In *The Moral Basis of Fielding's Art*, Martin C. Battestin has placed Fielding's Christianity within a tradition associated with the Latitudinarian divines of the middle and late seventeenth century. Such churchmen as Isaac Barrow, John Tillotson and Samuel Clarke preached a common-sense Christianity, putting emphasis on spiritual improvement through a good-natured perspective on life and on an active involvement with society. In contrast to those who emphasised man's fallen nature and the need for divine grace, the Latitudinarians spoke of the need to earn salvation through benevolence and good works. They felt that although man is fallen, there is an essential goodness in human nature which must be encouraged. Charity, love of neighbours and good-natured compassion for others were more important than religious knowledge or ritual. In *Joseph Andrews*, Joseph unconsciously acts with benevolence and Parson Adams both acts according to and preaches this doctrine.

John Wesley

John Wesley (1703–91) was a Church reformer and one of the original Methodists. The Methodist emphasis on faith and grace was contrary to Fielding's Latitudinarian concern with charity and good works.

George Whitefield

George Whitefield (1714–70) was one of the Methodists who attempted to reform the Church of England. Whitefield's doctrines were at the time regarded as radical and he was forbidden to teach in the churches. While Fielding sympathised with Whitefield's desire for Church reform, he distrusted the emphasis in Methodism on faith in place of good works. As Parson Adams says, the doctrine of faith would have a 'pernicious Influence on Society' since a person could do evil but feel saved because he believed (Book I, Chapter 17). Such a separation of religious belief from social conduct appeared to destroy the foundations of Christian ethical behaviour that Fielding desired.

Colley Cibber

Colley Cibber's (1671–1757) autobiography was published in 1740. Cibber, a former actor and producer of plays, was notorious throughout the late seventeenth and early eighteenth centuries. He was a bad actor whose stage performances were sometimes hissed. He was a bad poet who through influence became Poet Laureate. Cibber was vigorously attacked by critics of his autobiography for its poor style, his arrogance, his self-publicising and his opinions. Like Walpole and Hervey, Cibber was one of those people who appeared to represent to others what was wrong with the era. He was felt to be pushing, incompetent and without taste or sense. He was used by Alexander Pope as the anti-hero of the 1743 *Dunciad*, who brings chaos and dullness to modern culture. In the *Champion* (Tuesday 29 April 1740) Fielding mockingly praises Cibber as 'one of the *Greatest Writers* of our Age' who shows '*we have frequently Great Writers that cannot read*'. Fielding then quotes passages of Cibber's writing, in which there are mistakes in grammar and vocabulary, as examples of how to be a great writer without the ability to read or write!

William Hogarth

William Hogarth (1697–1764), a well known painter and engraver, was a friend of Fielding. The gestures and symbolism of his paintings often are the visual equivalents of the descriptions and themes in *Joseph Andrews*.

Lord Hervey

Beau Didapper is partly based on John, Lord Hervey (1696–1743), an effeminate courtier, once a favourite of Queen Caroline and a strong member of Walpole's group in the House of Lords. Hervey, who was Vice-Chamberlain (1730) and Lord Privy Seal (1740), was notorious for his use of cosmetics and his love of French fashions. He is the original of Alexander Pope's character of Sporus in the *Epistle to Dr Arbuthnot*.

Peter Walker

Peter Pounce is based on Peter Walker (1664–1746), a notorious miser and moneylender, who was from 1715 to 1727 a Member of Parliament.

Part 4

Hints for study

Points for detailed study

To prepare for an examination or test or to write an essay, it is first necessary to feel at ease with the work you have studied. Read *Joseph Andrews*, then, after reading these Notes, re-read the novel. Pay particular attention to the narrative technique, the narrator, the structure, the characters, the themes and the style. Do not worry over the allusions in the footnotes of your edition. The allusions are additional entertainment for the eighteenth-century reader and those with a broad general education; they are not essential to a general understanding of the novel. It is unlikely, unless specifically lectured upon, that you will be tested on any exact knowledge concerning literary allusions, imitations or parodies. You should, however, have a general knowledge of what kind of material Fielding alludes to and the function of the imitations and parodies.

After you have re-read *Joseph Andrews*, review the topics below by writing a paragraph on each, summarising the points you might make if answering an examination question:

1. Narrative technique and structure:
(*a*) Comic epic in prose
(*b*) Imitation, parody and mock-heroic
(*c*) Structural parallels
(*d*) Contrasts
(*e*) Stereotyped descriptions and gestures
(*f*) The purpose of the narrator
(*g*) Distance
(*h*) Variety
(*i*) The Manner of Cervantes

2. Themes:
(*a*) Affectation
(*b*) Chastity
(*c*) Charity
(*d*) Self-interest
(*e*) High society
(*f*) The example of Pamela

(g) The clergy
(h) Eighteenth-century justice
(i) Faith and grace

3. Characters:
(a) The main characters: Joseph, Parson Adams, Fanny, Mrs Slipslop, Lady Booby
(b) Minor characters: Parson Barnabas, Parson Trulliber, Leonora, Mr Wilson, the pedlar
(c) Character types: for example, Beau Didapper, Lawyer Scout

Significant chapters

Give special attention to the chapters listed below. Study them carefully. Notice any speeches which describe Fielding's theory of art, narrative method or themes in the novel. Practise writing an essay analysing a chapter. Pay attention to how the events of the chapter are related to the main narrative of the novel. Preface; Book I, Chapter 1; Book 1 Chapter 12; Book II, Chapter 4; Book II, Chapter 6; Book II, Chapter 9; Book II, Chapter 12; Book III, Chapter 1; Book III, Chapter 3; Book III, Chapter 4; Book III, Chapter 11; Book IV, Chapter 8; Book IV, Chapter 16.

Sample questions and answers

Discuss and explain Book II, Chapter 12

Fanny and Joseph are first shown together slightly before the middle of the novel. This is the first of two scenes in which Fanny will be reunited with Joseph in an ale house. (In Book III, Chapter 12, she is brought to Joseph by Peter, who has saved her from the wicked captain.) The delay of the reunion of the lovers creates suspense and variety. Their reunion knits together the separate narratives of Adams and Fanny from the preceding chapters and contrasts to the situation that has developed between Joseph and Mrs Slipslop, who wants the young man for herself.

Fielding describes Fanny as beautiful but not perfect. She is full breasted and has large hips; her teeth are slightly uneven and she has a smallpox mark. She is also sunburnt. The portrait is of a lovely, healthy, young woman of nineteen, who is ripe for love. She is no slender fashion model; even her slight imperfections contribute to her sexual attractiveness. This impression is furthered by such descriptive words as 'plump', 'bursting', 'swelling' and 'moist'.

Joseph sings a typical Restoration song, probably learned when he was living in London, in which there are allusions to sexual pleasure. The poem offers a parallel to the situation. It concerns a man separated from the woman he loves, whom he cannot forget. He sees her, seizes her and whispers that they are alone. The conclusion of the poem plays on the word 'expiring', to mean the highest sexual pleasure ('to die' being the usual seventeenth-century expression), and the somewhat surprising change of register when Chloe replies that Stephen was never 'so pressing before'. 'Pressing' has the meaning of 'demanding', but puns on the physical implications of the scene described in the song.

The separated lovers, the man carrying the woman's image in his mind, the attraction she holds for others, who press their advances on her, the surprise reunion and the subsequent seizing and kissing of the beloved are all echoes or reflections of the relationship between Joseph and Fanny. Joseph clasps his beloved in his arms and they begin kissing, but unlike the lovers of the song, they are not alone and their bliss comes to a conclusion when Fanny recovers her modesty.

Fielding's language in the two paragraphs following the kisses of the lovers is filled with words and phrases suggesting the passion the two lovers feel: 'lusciousness', 'rapture of joy', 'first tumults' and 'impetuosity of her transports'. When Parson Adams recovers his manuscript from the fire where it 'lay expiring', there is a further reminder of the joys felt by the young lovers. Although it is not explicitly stated, it is likely that Mrs Slipslop refuses to return Fanny's curtsey and pretends she does not know her because she is jealous of the scene she has witnessed.

The chapter is carefully presented. It begins with a contrast between the storm raging outside and the calm within the house. In the second paragraph the narrator speaks of Pygmalion and Narcissus and 'Lady ____'s image'; both Narcissus' and Chloe's images are mentioned in the poem. The portrait of Fanny shows that she is 'bursting' with womanliness. In saving himself for her Joseph is no weak, bloodless puritan; she is sexually attractive and has various features that former ages considered signs of a passionate nature (such as black eyes, moist lips, and full hips). After we are told that Fanny has a 'natural gentility, superior to the acquisitions of art', the song that follows seems artificial, but in fact summarises the situation that next develops. When Fanny faints after hearing the singer's voice, the reader will probably feel pleasure in being suddenly reminded that Joseph was an accomplished singer. Fielding then modestly shifts our attention from the lovers to Parson Adams's and Mrs Slipslop's reactions to the scene. The chapter ends with a reminder of Adams's eccentricity, a demonstration of Fanny's natural modesty and the comedy of a jealous Mrs Slipslop pretending that she does not know Joseph's beloved. This modulation into another key leads Fielding into the next chapter with its humorous 'dissertation' on the absurdity of snobbery and airs of superiority. Chapter 12 offers a well rounded and proportioned scene which advances our understanding of Joseph and Fanny's love for each other.

Discuss the relationship of the story of Mr Wilson to the main plot

Mr Wilson's history might be described as a didactic tale aimed against the vices of fashionable society. His young manhood is a typical rake's progress. Heir to a fortune, he experiments with all vices until, impoverished and imprisoned, disenchanted with love, ignored by all his old friends, he is saved by a kind and virtuous woman whom he marries. They retire from the temptations of the city to the countryside where they live, happily married, with their children. In Book III, Chapter 4, it is implied that their life is a return to Eden. Their garden is without fashionable ornaments; they live simply; they grow their own food. Mr Wilson and his wife enjoy each other's company and the company of their children. They make their own wine and beer, keep no servants and practise charity towards their neighbours. Adams says this is how people lived in the 'golden age'.

Mr Wilson's history first shows the dangers to a young man of having money without moral guidance. 'And to this early introduction into life, without a guide, I impute all my future misfortune.' The 'roasting squire' (Book III, Chapter 7) is another instance of someone raised without a moral education, who grows up to be wicked. Both might be seen in contrast to the guidance that Parson Adams provided Joseph as a youth. Wilson is similar to Joseph in enjoying the various fashions of London on his arrival there, but unlike Joseph he takes to vices and indulges himself with prostitutes and other easily available women. He also ruins an innocent, beautiful young woman, who eventually becomes a prostitute. As Wilson proceeds downwards, wasting his money and life, he meets all the rudeness and dishonesty of fashionable London society. He is insulted by the great, cheated, and arrested for non-payment of debts. His fate is an example of what Joseph's might have been if he had not had Parson Adams's moral and religious guidance while young.

When Mr Wilson's life changes, after he is rescued from prison by a woman whom he loves, his retirement from the city to the countryside and his love and fidelity to his wife might be said to be a foreshadowing of Joseph's future happiness with Fanny. The novel will end with Joseph living a happily retired married life with his wife and children, as a farmer.

Mr Wilson's history also serves another function in the novel besides offering variety, a moral story and providing various parallels and contrasts to the main story. We are told that he lost a son, and in Book IV the son is discovered to be Joseph. The two stories are thus surprisingly linked; although Mr Wilson's history at first appears to be a digression, it is finally seen as a significant part of the novel.

Discuss the contrast between London and the country in Joseph Andrews

The city is often associated in people's minds with sophisticated vices, while the countryside is felt to be the place where there are traditional values, an older way of life and moral goodness. A theme common to many works of literature is the contrast between the temptations of city life and the innocence of the countryside. Fielding makes use of this contrast in *Joseph Andrews*. Joseph's journey, which occupies over half the novel, is from the corruption of London towards a happy marriage with Fanny Goodwill in the country, where he will lead a life of retirement.

Joseph is taken to London by Mrs Booby as a personal servant. In London he meets other young men who attempt to persuade him that his moral scruples are wrong. They 'game, swear, drink'. Joseph writes to Pamela: 'London is a bad place, and there is so little good fellowship, that next-door neighbours don't know one another.' Lady Booby, who was educated in London, mistakes Joseph's fashionable appearance for a knowledge of the world, and attempts to seduce him. She is shocked when he speaks of his virtue. Lady Booby was 'bless'd with a town education and never spoke of any of her country neighbours by any other appellation than that of brute'. She feels that Joseph lacks 'spirit' but under the influence of London he will show *'some life'*. In London she walks with him in Hyde Park, has him bring messages to her bedroom, and begins to treat him as a pet whom she expects to take for a lover.

Although Joseph fails to be tempted by big city ways, Mr Wilson wastes his inheritance in London on clothes, women and entertainment. In contrast to such citified behaviour, there is the countryside where Mr Wilson retires with his wife to live in 'the manner in which people had lived in the golden age'. After his marriage Joseph purchases 'a little estate in the same parish with his father', where he lives happily imitating the retirement of his parents from high society.

While a rural life of gardening, farming and a closely knit family is the implied ideal in *Joseph Andrews*, the countryside is not free from vice. In their journey throughout the countryside, Joseph, Fanny and Adams meet more than enough proud and villainous characters to show that there is vanity and corruption in the country as well as in the city. It is, however, in the country where it is possible to live naturally and innocently, away from the affectation and temptation of fashionable behaviour. It is only in the country where one can live in the manner of the 'golden age'.

Part 5

Suggestions for further reading

The text

Joseph Andrews, edited by Martin C. Battestin, Oxford University Press, Oxford, 1967. This is the standard modern edition, and part of 'The Wesleyan Edition of the Works of Henry Fielding'

The History of the Adventures of Joseph Andrews and *An Apology for the Life of Mrs Shamela Andrews*, edited by Douglas Brooks, Oxford University Press, Oxford, 1970. This is based on Battestin's edition, with additional, but fewer annotations, but a more interpretative introduction

Joseph Andrews, edited by R.F. Brissenden, Penguin Books, Harmondsworth, 1977, 1978. Also based on Battestin's edition, this is the text to which these Notes refer.

Other works by Henry Fielding

Tom Jones, Penguin Books, Harmondsworth, 1966
Jonathan Wild, Everyman's Library, London and New York, 1932
Amelia, Everyman's Library, London and New York, 2 vols, 1930

Works on Fielding

BATTESTIN, MARTIN C.: *The Moral Basis of Fielding's Art: A Study of 'Joseph Andrews'*, Wesleyan University Press, Middletown, Conn., 1959. An influential study of the religious and cultural background of the novel

BUTT, JOHN: *Fielding* (Writers and their Work), Longman, Green & Co., for the British Council, London, revised 1959. A good brief introduction

GOLDBERG, HOMER: *The Art of 'Joseph Andrews'*, University of Chicago Press, Chicago, 1969. Aspects of the novel, its tradition, and Fielding's intentions

JOHNSON, MAURICE: *Fielding's Art of Fiction*, University of Pennsylvania Press, Philadelphia, 1961, 1965. Eleven essays on Fielding's novels, which have influenced subsequent critics

PAULSON, RONALD (ED.): *Fielding: A Collection of Critical Essays: Twentieth-Century Views*, Prentice Hall, Englewood Cliffs, N.J., 1962. A republication of the main modern critical opinions

PAULSON, RONALD and LOCKWOOD, THOMAS (ED): *Henry Fielding: The Critical Heritage*, Routledge and Kegan Paul, London, 1969. The contemporary sources quoted in Part 1 of these Notes and other eighteenth-century judgements of Fielding are printed in this useful book

RAWSON, C.J.: *Henry Fielding and the Augustan Ideal Under Stress*, Routledge and Kegan Paul, London, 1972. Unconventional essays on aspects of Fielding's novels. A rather specialised study

RAWSON, CLAUDE (ED.): *Henry Fielding: A Critical Anthology*, Penguin Books, Harmondsworth, 1973. The fullest selection of critical opinion from the eighteenth century to the present

SACKS, SHELDON: *Fiction and the Shape of Belief: a Study of Henry Fielding*, University of California Press, Los Angeles and Berkeley, 1966. An advanced study; an attempt to show how writers embody their values in literary forms

Background reading

ROGERS, PAT: *The Augustan Vision*, Methuen, London, 1978. A general introduction to the culture and literature of the period 1688–1760

ROGERS, PAT (ED.): *The Eighteenth Century*, Methuen, London, 1978. Essays on such topics as politics, science, the visual arts, religion, ideas and the writer and society

The author of these notes

BRUCE KING was educated at Columbia University and the University of Leeds. He has taught English at universities in the United States, Canada, England, Scotland, France and Nigeria. He is Professor of English at the University of Canterbury, New Zealand. His publications include *Dryden's Major Plays, Marvell's Allegorical Poetry*, and *New English Literatures*. He is also the author of the York Notes on Shaw's *Arms and Man* and Ibsen's *A Doll's House*.